The Literacy Toolkit

What an incredible resource this book is, enjoyable to read, passionately written, theoretically sound, yet firmly grounded in the realities of everyday school life and the world of the modern learner. This exciting, well-researched treasure-trove presents hundreds of creative classroom strategies to help you raise the literacy bar. For leaders and managers, there are plenty of well-conceived ideas for whole school development, cross-curricular literacy, staff training, monitoring and assessment. Whoever you are and whatever you teach, you are a member of your school's literacy development team; I'm sure that you will find Amanda's ideas illuminating, motivating and empowering.

Six key themes underpin the author's vision of a modern literacy curriculum. They are:

1. The ever-expanding world of mass communications directly affects how children and young adults learn about language.

2. Communications to and between children and young adults are increasingly multi-media, involving images, sound and text.

3. Oracy is the foundation of good literacy.

4. Well-designed cross-curricular approaches provide meaningful contexts for learning literacy skills and knowledge.

5. Helping students to become media and language 'savvy' will help them to develop into confident thinkers and willing lifelong learners.

6. The importance of being bold, brave and creative! Developing language and literacy skills should be a satisfying and joyful experience for all learners.

Sharon Ginnis, author of *Covering the Curriculum with Stories* and Independent Trainer

This is a timely, thorough and very practical book filled with approaches to literacy that can work in all sorts of classrooms with all sorts of learners. All teachers will find something of use here along with a reiteration of how literacy is right at the heart of what education should be all about—the opening up of worlds for young people.

Ian Gilbert, Founder of Independent Thinking Ltd

The Literacy Toolkit by Amanda Sara is a comprehensive book of literacy explanations and suggestions, which provides in depth knowledge about the importance of literacy in today's society. Whilst offering simple and effective strategies, which can be used in a wide range of curriculum subjects, this book highlights the importance that every teacher is a teacher of English. The literacy toolkit offers all teachers clear and specific guidelines on literacy learning activities and allows scope for all students to develop their literacy levels further.

Andrea Donovan, Spirit Whana, Dean of International Students, English teacher, HOD ESOL

An intelligent mix of substantiating theory and practical tasks. I will be buying a copy for my department resource library and, more importantly, using it!

Martin Back, Head of English/Staff Welfare Officer, Roedean School

The Literacy Toolkit is packed full of ideas which classroom teachers can use to inspire students to love words.

**Bill Lucas, Professor of Learning, University of Winchester and Trustee,
The English Project**

Anyone involved in education will know the immense value of high quality tools for teaching and learning. With this book Amanda has crafted a clear, compelling and useful toolkit for the most fundamental of issues.

Sebastian Bailey, The Mind Gym

The genius of Amanda Sara's *Literacy Toolkit* is that it satisfies the teacher and the student's intellectual curiosity whilst providing both with stimulating strategies to raise levels of literacy. Amanda embraces a definition of literacy that encompasses all its new technological forms and enables students to 'crack these codes' in ways that will develop and support all other learning and to assess progress.

Amanda's book will motivate teacher and student and actually allow both to enjoy creative, fun and purposeful activities.

**David Onllwyn-Jones MBE, Assistant Head Teacher, Villiers High School, West London
Teacher of the Year in a Secondary School in London 2006
Comenius Ambassador, British Council**

The Literacy Toolkit is a must-read for teachers, literacy coordinators and school leaders. It provides a one-stop resource for getting your school buzzing with literacy practice that will raise results and deepen learning. Based on up-to-date research about how learning really happens, all suggested practices are linked to the Learning to Learn and Assessment for Learning agendas. This book delivers a clear and integrated vision of what 21st century education should look like. Amanda clearly demonstrates that literacy is at the very heart of pushing education forward, underpinning not just achievement, but also enjoyment.

Not only providing background, research and educational vision, *The Literacy Toolkit* contains a wealth of practical, cross-curricular activities and resources for the classroom. For literacy co-ordinators it sets out clearly how to strategically plan and lead a whole-school approach, while tailoring it to the school's individual circumstances. A book of tricks to motivate and engage staff and students alike!

Fiona Tierney, Teacher Leader for Literacy, North Oxfordshire Academy

Michael Proust once said, 'I believe that reading, in its original essence, [is] that fruitful miracle of communication in the midst of solitude.' In *The Literacy Toolkit*, Sara reminds teachers of English that this type of communication happens regardless of the way one reads (beyond its original essence). For example, when watching a film, reading a picture, decoding words, listening to a book on tape or doing any of these things simultaneously—there is always a solitary communication that occurs. It happens also through writing. So part of the process of supporting literacy development is to help children become critical readers of the messages they will inevitably encounter and critical writers of the messages they will inevitably send and *The Literacy Toolkit* offers strategies to help achieve this.

**Laura Manni, Early Years Coordinator and Pre-School Teacher, American International
School of Lusaka and Director, Mukwashi Trust Primary School**

This book encapsulates all the essential tools a teacher in modern day education needs to inspire students to excel and improve their own speaking, listening, reading and writing skills. It brings to light some very important educational ideals that challenge pupils to develop skills in lifelong learning, based around literacy and its importance in modern day society. I would highly recommend any teacher looking for a unique framework of literacy tools to read this book and adapt its practices to their own curriculum needs thereby opening their students' minds to the literary crafts of speaking, listening, reading and writing.

He, who speaks not for the sake of speaking, but for the sake of being heard, will inspire those to write and read his message.

Mark Thomas Dixon, Physical Education Curriculum Enrichment Coordinator

This book provides an excellent balance of traditional theories, current thinking and practical activities. Teachers who would not necessarily think of themselves as 'experts' now have a handbook which they can use to brush up on their own literacy skills before standing in front of a class. The activities are engaging and will appeal to today's students and will provide an essential framework of skills, especially for EAL learners.

Paul Lees, Head of Teaching and Learning, The Winchester School, Dubai, UAE

It is perhaps advantageous that Amanda Sara's *The Literacy Toolkit* has appeared just when the emphasis in education has once again returned to literacy. Supported as it is by a mix of theory and practical advice, this seems a useful addition to a teacher's bookshelf. The text opens with its theoretical basis, which sets out a 'literacy' which is not dependent on the written word but acknowledges both oracy and visual literacy, mentioning multimedia texts with a familiarity of which the authors of the new curriculum would approve. There is, however, an emphasis on the secondary classroom which seems apt given the author's background.

Sara is able to talk convincingly about literacy and has the experience of both classroom practice and research to underpin her ideas.

The second section of the book which deals with practical activities to address literacy skills is fun and dominated by a sense of competition. It is important to mention the 'boy-friendly' nature of many of these activities and the use of metaphors which concentrate on different car and fuel types. Each activity is also framed by a quotation from a famous person/thinker which makes reading enjoyable for one such as myself.

The whole school emphasis of the final section of the text is interesting and takes the opportunity to reiterate several key points: one being the connection between being literate and being successful. Sara is able to demonstrate a passion for the subject beyond her own remit of English teacher and make a convincing argument for integrated and far-reaching approaches to raising the profile of literacy and reading within the curriculum. A major strength is the plethora of proformas and tables which are immediately of use for teachers, each activity is clearly explained but allows for the personalisation of tasks in order to suit a specific class or group. This is a useful text which would be a valuable addition to any teacher's professional library.

Carol Verity, Secondary English Consultant, London Borough of Ealing

The Literacy Toolkit delivers a very clear message and is clearly based on a thorough appreciation of modern day research which includes significant reference to government and Department for Children, Schools and Families policies and initiatives. These references, however, whilst useful and contextually pertinent, are not the key strengths of this work. What is presented is a series of simple yet effective strategies and practical examples that can be used and manipulated in a variety of different contexts to help focus the attention of young people to appreciate language and the means by which they can acquire a greater command of it.

All too often in works that focus on literacy, too much space is given to identifying the issues and much less focus is given to providing practical solutions; not so *The Literacy Toolkit*. By focusing on three key questions: 'What is literacy about?', 'How are you going to overcome resistance?' and 'What do you want children to be able to do as a result of achieving better literacy skills?', Amanda Sara not only provides a relevant, useful and accessible commentary, but she also provides a host of practical solutions that will help stimulate the imagination and the purposeful engagement of learners.

Regardless of the subject taught, *The Literary Toolkit* will help teachers to support their pupils in being better learners by providing useful methods for them to acquire and deploy language in a meaningful and productive manner. Herein lies one of the means by which we can help turn pupils into real learners and active participants in society and not just whilst they are at school. *The Literacy Toolkit* is less an academic tome than a very practical and worthwhile volume for all classroom practitioners.

Gino Carminati, Head Teacher, Worth School

Drawing on her years of experience as teacher, mentor and literacy adviser, the author sets out first the principles and theories of literacy and literacy development, then offers fifty strategies, all of which can be modified and personalised to particular subjects and groups of students, before offering advice and guidance on whole school or whole department/year group strategies.

As the author says, 'Imagine a school in which every student loved to read, loved to talk, loved to write.' This book will help any school in moving closer to that ambition. 'Begin the journey now. Together we can make a difference.'

Al Grant, Assistant Headteacher, Elthorne Park High School, Ealing, London

The Literacy Toolkit is a very good resource of cross curricular activities to promote literacy skills and encourage staff to embed literacy skills in all areas of learning. The range of scenarios and activities will enable and motivate staff and students from all backgrounds to value literacy skills to improve engagement and achievement. This is a very good resource for literacy specialists, and non-specialists, in schools and colleges to gain ideas to promote literacy with the functional skills agenda.

John T Morris, JTM Educational Consultants

The Literacy Toolkit

Improving students' speaking, listening, reading and writing skills

Amanda Sara

Illustrations by Helen Clare Brienza

Crown House Publishing Limited
www.crownhouse.co.uk
www.crownhousepublishing.com

First published by

Crown House Publishing Ltd
Crown Buildings, Bancyfelin, Carmarthen, Wales, SA33 5ND, UK
www.crownhouse.co.uk

and

Crown House Publishing Company LLC
6 Trowbridge Drive, Suite 5, Bethel, CT 06801-2858, USA
www.crownhousepublishing.com

First published 2009. Reprinted 2011.

British Library Cataloguing in Publication Data
A catalogue entry for this book is available from the British Library.

13-digit ISBN 978-1845901325
LCCN 2008936796

Printed and bound in the UK by
Bell & Bain Limited, Glasgow

Dedicated to Pauline, Basil, Jonathan and Nan.

Foreword

Over the last 20 years or so there have been major changes in what is seen as 'literacy'. We are now very familiar with reading material where pictures and design features accompany—and sometimes outweigh—print. All forms of public texts are more image-based. Of course, newspapers and magazines have included pictures for a long time but now financial and commercial documents also use images and designed text to get their messages across and information texts of all kinds are more visually presented. Although we can be sure that books and other printed materials will not be displaced, the new literacy made possible by the digital revolution has implications for education. Reading now has to take into account new forms of text made possible by technology and, in particular, the screen. Texting, emails, blogs and twittering are part of young people's daily experience, bringing a new range of writing to the traditional repertoire. Sound, too, is taking a more prominent position, not only in the ubiquitous mobile phone but often as background sound in visual texts and in expectations that students should be able to communicate ideas orally with clarity and conviction. In addition, literacy has taken a more global turn, and it is becoming more important to be able to speak more than one language. Young people who have English as an additional language strengthen their potential to respond to globalisation. In all its aspects, literacy now has a much wider range than before, and that places responsibilities on all those who are involved in education.

Young people bring a wide experience of visual, spoken and multimedia texts to their school work, expecting to read images as well as print and to use computers in seeking information and composing their own texts. Many of these texts combine words with moving images, sound, colour, a range of photographic, drawn or digitally created visuals; some are interactive, encouraging the reader to compose, represent ideas and communicate through the several dimensions offered by the technology. If this wealth of experience is to be used as a basis for further learning, it is important that literacy provision in schools acknowledges and uses students' varied text experience. *The Literacy Toolkit* places school literacy in the context of the new literacy, offering a wealth of ideas about how talk and the visual can be seen as important components in developing successful reading and writing with a diverse range of young people. Firmly grounded in classroom experience, the tried and tested ideas are based on awareness of how literacy is best developed. The scope is wide and innovative, giving solid practical advice to any teacher or any school committed to developing an approach to literacy across the curriculum which will open up a wider perspective of what being a fully developed reader, writer, speaker and listener can mean.

Dr Eve Bearne
Past President of the United Kingdom Literacy Association

Preface

Welcome to *The Literacy Toolkit*. In the following pages you will find information on tools and strategies that I have used successfully to help raise literacy levels in schools and academies.

Raising literacy levels is not the remit of English department teachers alone. It is a target that we as teachers, across all age groups and subject areas, have to address in varying levels of complexity. Ideally, we all want a resource (or two) that allows us to locate strategies that will work (or can be adapted to work) with a range of students in a range of settings; strategies that address the literacy issues teachers encounter every day.

The Literacy Toolkit: Improving Students' Speaking, Listening, Reading and Writing Skills is a journey into understanding literacy in our society, its impact upon our schools and the practical and creative strategies we can use to develop literacy in all subjects. It embraces what we know about literacy learning and demonstrates how we can move things forward creatively in the classroom and beyond, so that students, learners and teachers can have a positive impact upon learning.

It also highlights the notion that literacy needs to be addressed by all, in order for all students to succeed. It looks at the key issues and approaches needed to address literacy in a creative, fun and purposeful manner.

The principles that underpin *The Literacy Toolkit* are accessible for all teachers to adopt. They are divided into four chapters:

1. Literacy in our society – the importance of it and how we put that into practice in our schools.

2. Fifty generic literacy strategies for teachers to use in the classroom.

3. Whole school literacy strategies:
   * Effective literacy
   * Leading cross-curricular literacy, training staff, monitoring outcomes and assessment
   * All staff involvement in developing literacy across the curriculum
   * Using ICT and media to develop students' literacy
   * The role of oracy in form time to transform literacy
   * The role of reading in developing and raising literacy
   * The role of writing in developing and raising literacy
   * The role of EAL in transforming literacy
   * Level 3 learners and transforming their learning through literacy
   * The role of parents in transforming literacy
   * Boys and literacy

4. A selection of generic tools that can to be used to assess literacy development .

By weaving these strategies together this book provides a supportive toolkit for schools and should increase student motivation to master literacy.

I hope you enjoy using *The Literacy Toolkit* as much as I have enjoyed my journey writing it.

Amanda J. Sara
London

Acknowledgements

My deepest thanks to all my family and friends for your love and support.

My parents, Pauline and Basil—this is for you with love.

Jonathan, for proofreading this with a smile.

Sophie, Amber, Catherine, Maeve, Laura, Jo, Nan!

Cecilia Payton, Caroline Cuinet Wellings, Helen McGrath for becoming an extension of my family.

For my second family at Cambridge, Clare College—Professor Badger, Dr Tony Bower and Dr Eve Bearne for your encouragement, love and support in moulding my research mind.

My deepest thanks also goes to (in no particular order) the following people/organisations who have all helped me tremendously:

The Royal Society of Arts for welcoming me so warmly as a Fellow for my literacy work.

Paul Ginnis, Sharon Ginnis, Bill Watkin, the Specialist Schools and Academies Trust, Crown House Publishing, Dai Jones, Sebastian Bailey, Worth School, St Mary's Hall, Roedean School, Westminster Academy, North Oxfordshire Academy.

The staff, present and past, and pupils at Villiers High School, Southall for allowing me to grow as a teacher.

Bethan Marshall for opening the door to the world of English teaching.

Dr Eve Bearne, Laura Manni and Jonathan Sara for editing.

There are so many other people to thank, please know that even if you are not mentioned here you are in my heart.

Contents

Foreword   ix
Preface   xi
Acknowledgements   xiii
List of abbreviations   xvii

Chapter 1: Introduction to Literacy   1

Chapter 2: 50 Generic Strategies for Literacy Teaching   19
  1. Root words   20
  2. Capital letters and full stops   22
  3. Dictionaries   24
  4. Learning and remembering spellings   26
  5. Speech and quotes   28
  6. Homophones   30
  7. Connectives – How far can you run?   33
  8. Vocabulary size   35
  9. Thesauruses   38
 10. Paragraphs   41
 11. Apostrophe snap!   44
 12. Proofreading   46
 13. Herringbone Pattern   48
 14. Sentences   50
 15. Make me an author! Are you an author or an editor?   52
 16. Notes   54
 17. Past, present and future questions   55
 18. Prediction   57
 19. Skimming and scanning   59
 20. Book corner   61
 21. Window shopping!   62
 22. Crosswords and Sudoku   63
 23. Roll the dice!   65
 24. Circles cascade!   67
 25. What's your problem?   68
 26. Finding the clues   69
 27. Guided writing – What do I need?   70
 28. Writing frame – Writing a balanced argument   74
 29. Writing to argue   76

30. Writing frame – Writing instructions 78
31. Persuasive writing 80
32. Writing to explain 83
33. Writing to recount 85
34. Writing to advise 87
35. Instant response 89
36. Annotating 90
37. Writing frame for story writing 91
38. Speaking through finger puppets 93
39. Circle – Who am I? 95
40. Presentations 97
41. Literacy chairs 99
42. Freeze-frame 101
43. Las Vegas – Clap and roll the dice 103
44. Let's speak all week! 104
45. Diplomats 108
46. Rise from the dead – Become a specialist of your subject 110
47. Questions – Open and closed 112
48. Weather corners 114
49. Voicemail! 117
50. United students! 119

Chapter 3: Whole School Strategies **121**

Effective literacy 122
Leading cross-curricular literacy, training staff, monitoring outcomes
and assessment 123
All staff involvement in developing literacy across the curriculum 128
Using ICT and media to develop students' literacy 131
The role of oracy in form time to transform literacy 133
The role of reading in developing and raising literacy 143
The role of writing in developing and raising literacy 146
The role of EAL in transforming literacy 149
Level 3 learners and transforming their learning through literacy 151
The role of parents in transforming literacy 153
Boys and literacy 154

Chapter 4: Generic Tools for Assessing Literacy **159**

Bibliography 169
Index 173

List of abbreviations

BFI – British Film Institute

CILIP – Chartered Institute of Library and Information Professionals

CLPE – Centre for Literacy in Primary Education

DARTS – Directed Activities Related to Text

EAL – English as an Additional Language

IB – International Baccalaureate

ICT – Information Communication Technology

MYB – Middle Years Baccalaureate

NIFTC – Northern Ireland Film and Television Commission

NQTs – Newly Qualified Teachers

PIRLS – Progress in International Reading Literacy Study

PYB – Primary Years Baccalaureate

SPG – Spelling Punctuation Grammar

RSA – Royal Society of Arts

SSAT – Specialist Schools and Academies Trust

TAs – Teaching Assistants

UNESCO – United Nations Educational, Scientific and Cultural Organization

Please note: for ease of reading, when referring to male or female I have simply used 'their' throughout the book.

Literacy unlocks the door to learning throughout life.

Kofi Annan (1938–), former Secretary General of the United Nations,
awarded the Nobel Peace Prize

Chapter 1
Introduction to Literacy

Your relationship with books

> *One day, when I was eighteen, I was reading a book and I began to weep. I*
> *was astounded. I'd had no idea that literature could affect me in such a way.*
>
> Keith Johnstone, *Impro: Improvisation and the Theatre* (1979)

Take a moment and think about the role that books have played in your life. For example, have you ever read a book and found yourself ...

- laughing out loud?
- crying?
- angry?
- sad?
- shocked?
- having an 'Aha!' experience?
- fantasising about a life that you'd like to have?

What is it about a book that produces a significant state of change in the reader? Passion.

Good books are about passion—the author has something to tell you about their passion. And it could be anything from Formula 1 Racing to cooking. And in telling you about their passion, they will be telling you a story. For example, Jeremy Clarkson and Rick Stein are passionate people who tell fascinating stories. That's what it's all about—stories. Stories are what hold our society together, what hold our relationships together, what hold our sense of self together—we exist in the stories that we tell ourselves about who we are.

In the oral tradition of the past, people told stories and listeners remembered them. Then along came writing and the possibility of recording stories so that people who were not present could also 'hear' them. Nowadays there are relatively few storytellers who go by that name, but there are a huge number of storytellers in our society under different names—journalists, novelists, film-makers, the bloggerati, advertisers … In other words, we live in a storytelling culture and many of these stories are now written down. Therefore, in order to be able to contribute to our society, it is necessary to be able to write our own stories and to be able to read those of others. And not only read the words—but read between the lines, to find out more about the probable intentions of the writers.

> - The primary communication acts in our culture are spoken.
> - Literature is a way of recording speech acts for posterity, for people not present at the time, as well as to tell stories about human nature and histories about the progress of culture.
> - In other words, the spoken word comes first—the written forms are our way of holding a complex reality so that it can be shared by others.

You are obviously literate as you are reading this book. And there will have been many books you have read before this one. So as you think back to those books which have been significant in your life, notice which book or books, films or other stories:

- have changed your life;
- you have read or watched over and over until you knew them almost word-for-word or image-for-image;
- you have enthusiastically recommended to your friends;
- gave you a new understanding into the particular way you do things, so that you never had to do them again in that way;
- gave you insights into the way you relate to other people, so that you were able to be with them in a different way.

Now wouldn't it be great if all the children that you come into contact with were able to have similar experiences in their lives?

This is one of the stated aims of education—and a measure of the effectiveness of any kind of education is the degree to which those who are educated are able to have these kinds of experiences.

Definition of literacy

- The ability to create and to make sense of symbolic forms of communication, which refers to that which is not-here and not-now.
- The ability to encode and decode messages that enable appropriate interventions to be made in the world that will change the way things are.
- In other words: literacy is about the ability to take action based on information.
- For literature and entertainment (stories, novels, films) the action may be to understand the nature of what it is to be human; to understand human motivation, decision-making, relationships, imagination—for example, to understand something of the nature of love and loss.
- For information, the action is being able to know what things are and how they are to be used—for example, to read and understand the instructions for using a computer program and to know why and when it should be used.

So what's the problem?

How do you spell *inept?*

Despite government and educational programmes to increase literacy among young people, there is little evidence that literacy rates are increasing. The new Key Stage 3 curriculum is a reflection of education in today's society and how even as educators we are continually growing and learning. It is a reflection of the latest educational developments and ways in which we can take our students more effectively towards learning. The curriculum document aims to enable all students to develop into more successful learners: confident and sensible individuals who will have a positive impact upon our society.

The new curriculum:

- Emphasises a greater learning entitlement and higher standards for all students.
- Highlights the importance of progression, personalised learning, assessment and clarity, and promotes educational awareness among all members of society.
- Looks to raise standards in all subjects, especially Maths and English.
- Attempts to inspire and stimulate students' interests in their focus subjects, and so encourage them to strive for further education.
- Allows students to develop the learning to learn skills they need for their school and career and more generally in their journey through life.

One of the aims of the new national curriculum is to improve students' literacy through personalised learning (both inside and outside the classroom) and personalised assessment, which maximises the use of specialist staff and ensures that literacy is taught as part of all subject areas. That's where *The Literacy Toolkit* comes in. The majority of this book is dedicated to providing practical strategies and suggestions that can be used to promote literacy across the curriculum in your school.

Chapter 1 looks at the history of the literacy process in greater depth and provides the background and foundation knowledge required for Chapters 2, 3 and 4.

> *To be literate we have to be confident that the world of signs and print, in all the different mixtures and modes of meaning that surround us, is a world we can cope with, be at home in, contribute to and play with.*

Margaret Meek, *On Being Literate* (1991: 238)

Literacy is made up of several parts, including vocabulary, reading of all text types, writing and speaking, and presenting. According to Hall (2003: 2) there are four key learning perspectives. These are psycho-linguistic, cognitive-psychological, socio-cultural and socio-political.

Hall argues that it is important we 'resist attempts to polarize and pigeon-hole' these perspectives. It is our responsibility, as teachers, to embrace all four areas to ensure that our teaching includes opportunities to develop. Let's look more closely at the four perspectives.

1. Psycho-linguistic

This approach encourages teachers and students to immerse themselves in any book/text as long as the text is used to aid the teaching of reading and literacy. The emphasis is on reading (to read) rather than reading books on a prescribed reading list. The emphasis of this perspective encompasses the holistic approach which could be embraced more in schools—the merging of the book, the student and the teacher to ensure an interactive, meaningful learning experience, thereby maximising literacy learning.

2. Cognitive-psychological

This perspective looks at the teaching of word recognition and students' response to words in print. It highlights the importance of the structured teaching of phonics that is needed for children to tackle new words. Ironically, we have gone full circle with phonics and the debate about how it should and shouldn't be taught. The structured teaching of phonics has now become a key factor in the Primary National Strategy as a way to raise literacy levels.

3. Socio-cultural

This approach does not separate reading and writing from context. It is clear that children's language is a reflection of their cultural and social influences (e.g. birthday cards, magazines, newspapers, story books, holy texts). It is important that we recognise that children begin school with a wealth of literacy experiences and we must learn to utilise and accommodate this knowledge, as is now being highlighted by the media literacy focus in the new Key Stage 3 national curriculum.

4. Socio-political

This approach refers to the connection of literacy with power and challenging dependencies and inequalities. This echoes the words of the cross-curricular dimensions in the new Key Stage 3 curriculum—that students need to be aware of themselves, as well as the society they are a part of, in order to maximise their learning and literacy levels. The new Key Stage 3 national curriculum takes on board these areas by reshaping the curriculum for our students' futures, which hopefully will lead to an improvement in literacy levels.

It is also important to consider the research of Luke and Freebody (1997), who for the last few years have been telling us that when it comes to raising the standards of literacy, specifically reading, there are four categories to consider:

1. Coding practices – the reader developing the skills to unravel the text, patterns and conventions, irrespective of subject.
2. Text-meaning practices – developing the reader's skills to participate in the text by recognising the ideas, cultural resources and meanings in the text and how they interweave.
3. Pragmatic practices – the reader as a text user, with the ability to look at text composition and relate it to the present day.
4. Critical practices – text analysis and critique.

These categories are not intended to be mutually exclusive. To maximise their impact it is necessary to draw on the key elements from each and to help children recognise their interconnectedness in the process of reading and writing. If we only draw from and provide opportunities for children to develop in one area, we are not catering for the literacy needs of all our students.

Looking at the research of Hall and Luke and Freebody, it is clear that for literacy to succeed in today's society, we need to embrace it in all contexts.

It is often said that children who begin reading before they start their school life have greater and quicker literacy development. It is worth noting that early insight into looking, reading and being read to leads to greater progress in literacy later on in school life.

While we learn to read, we draw on different knowledge and experience—narrative, social, semantic, cultural and linguistic. It is easy to see that children are quick to engage in the phonic system and seem to enjoy seeing patterns and their names in letters—because it's fun! As teachers, we often use this to stimulate children's reading interest. Yet CLPE (1991) refer to this as 'the orchestration of knowledge'—the ability to draw upon all skills, such as reading words and an understanding of book print.

He's got a bright future.

Similarly, Meek (1991) highlights that learning to read and developing literacy skills is a complex process that requires the integration of imagination, thought, feeling and language. It is of note that often children read and make sense of narrative without being taught about it. This leads young children to engage in play which can result in make-believe and stories—thereby leading them back to reading and therefore developing their literacy skills to feed their imaginations. As Hardy (1977) found, children's desire to make up stories can lead them to read and enjoy the written text. The research of Bennett (1991) and Waterland (1988) also highlights the importance of picture books in children's learning, which aid in learning to read and helping to develop the visual imagination. This encourages play and ultimately returns children to reading and the development of literacy skills.

So, with these key parts of research in mind we can see where we are in relation to the past and where we want to go with the new national curriculum.

Many children do not read books—whilst we as adults think they should, because we read books and find them informative, useful and entertaining. We live in a society which is dependent upon literate members who are able to communicate effectively and whose livelihoods depend upon the ability to communicate well with one another.

Some children are not familiar with the process of extracting information from books or printed material, nor how to organise the thoughts and ideas of others in a way which makes sense to them. That is, they find it hard to make meaning from communications by others that fits in with their worldview and which enables them to take appropriate action as a consequence.

Why is this a problem?

If children do not have reading ability, they will be at a great disadvantage in a society that is heavily language and text-based.

What will happen if we do nothing or fail to resolve this problem?

Children will be frustrated that they cannot join in fully with society and are likely to become resentful.

How did things get to be this way?

Essentially, greater understanding of the psychological brain processes involved in learning to read needs to be shared with all teachers. Steven Pinker (2007) suggests teaching reading to children by first getting them to learn all the letters and sounds, and when this is done combining these together to pronounce whole words. This way each week a child will learn six new sounds. He argues that we are equipped to deal with language—we just have to nurture and develop our tools. Diana McGuinness (2005) is a firm believer in this approach and argues that children must learn the connection between letters and sounds. However, this is only part of how reading develops (because it also needs meaning as well as sounds).

What can we do in the future that is different?

By encouraging students to become critically literate, we are encouraging them to question what they see and read, whether it is words or images. Barthes (1986: 30) considers the various multimodal and multimedia texts available to us: 'Language … and image are in complementary relation; the words are then fragments … as are the images, and the message's unity occurs on a higher level.'

Only when words and images unite can students experience maximum understanding. Together they complement each other and this is what must be acknowledged—not that words and images are in competition with each other. After all, by interweaving one with the other they generally enhance students' overall literacy understanding.

It is worth noting that the study of literature now includes many different written print-based and visual screen-based text types—hence the constant de-construction and re-construction. Books provide children with an opportunity to learn the skills of reading and also mould them into the type of reader they will become in the future. Yet students read less the older they get, which mirrors the *majority* of adults' reading habits (although I have noticed from my own research that there is a tendency for girls and young children to re-read books). At the ages of 10, 12 and 14 only a minority of students read fiction and children spend more time watching television than reading, with boys watching more TV than girls. There is a suggestion that an interest in multimedia texts may trigger a greater interest in books.

Bearne (2003b) maintains that: 'moving images in film and television … are now part of children's everyday reading diet.'

This raises the issue of what reading means or how people perceive it. Bearne argues that the reading of different kinds of texts is important in contemporary culture. For example, comic books allow children to acquire an insight into how different language styles work for humour, including puns, alliteration, jokes, intertextuality, a range of voices (narrator, sound effects, characters) and multi-layered meaning. Thus, comics can be perceived as offering an important contribution to reading—especially shared reading, as they are often seen as having an interactive nature. Perhaps what needs to be emphasised is that because of the complicated layout, the skills required for comic book reading are challenging. Moreover, comics aimed at children aged between 10 and 13 use complex and sometimes technical language. Comics such as *The Beano* allow children to develop their reading not only by the intricate demands of the combination of words and images, but also by offering opportunities to research further information into the history of the magazine through puzzles, games and news reviews on an interactive website (www.beanotown.com). Thus, the official *Beano* website encourages children to read through both the written word texts and visual picture texts.

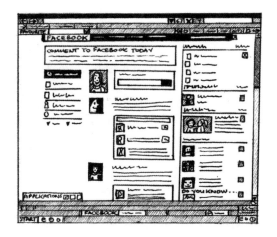

My research (Sara 2006) reveals that children today spend less time reading books and more time playing computer games and watching television. However, it also shows that children are 'reading' the images in order to understand what to do next when playing computer games, particularly as narrative is important in most games. Players have written instructions and a background history for the characters is provided, so they are still required to read screen-based written text. In some schools, students are being encouraged to play computer games in order to develop their literacy skills. The benefits are that it allows them to discuss ways to solve problems and give one another instructions by reading the narrative. Also computer glossaries encourage children to increase their vocabulary. Thus, computer games increase children's knowledge of language and literature skills as often they deal with sentence level, plot, narrative and characterisation (DfES 1997).

In a simple definition of visual literacy, Considine (1986: 38) suggests: 'Visually literate students should be able to produce and interpret visual images.' Advertising, such as signs, labels and posters, combine images and written texts and allow students to consider the interplay of both at work, as well as being alert to the language used. The internet and mobile phones are other forms of media with which children today engage. Both are becoming ubiquitous methods of communication and ways to acquire information. These add to the numerous text types which children are subjected to on a daily basis, and thereby add to their understanding and reading of various text types.

It is worth re-emphasising that in today's society, where technology is abundant, children are active users of computers, videos, mobile phones and digital cameras (to name but a few). As children are influenced by their exposure to these technologies, so their literacy is evolving. I feel that society is beginning to accept changes to the definition of literacy and is allowing for the integration of the influence of technology.

Visual texts are not alternatives to written texts but are a complement, and together they allow students to work towards their potential. Refusing to immerse students in a variety of text types is to suppress their learning. The constant de-constructing and re-constructing of literature is an important part of the new multimodal landscape that has emerged and incorporated itself into the curriculum. Vygotsky (1962) claims that children make their own sense of the world they live in, yet they need knowledgeable adults to nurture their thinking and actions. Today it is technology that acts as a surrogate mediator. So, technology and adults together are shaping the literature of children whether it is through print-based or screen-based texts.

Who needs to take action?

All teachers, regardless of specialism.

What has the government done to change the teaching of reading?

Primary education in the United Kingdom is very good and compares well internationally. The new Primary Literacy Strategy builds on the success we have achieved and offers us further tools as teachers and leaders.

The Every Child A Reader programme highlights some of the fundamental issues in the Every Child Matters and Personalisation agendas. The programme offers students with severe reading issues daily one-to-one reading with 'reading recovery' teachers. In addition, students with less acute reading difficulties are offered interventions such as Fischer Family Trust Wave 3, Better Reading Partnership and Early Literacy Support. One of the developments of the revised strategy is the evidence of emersion into literature.

It is clear that the teaching of reading has shifted to a back-to-basics method of synthetic phonics, as recommended by the Rose Review in 2005. The new national curriculum requires students to study numerous cultures and traditions at all key stages, ranging from poems and stories of various cultures in Year 1 to a variety of text types in Year 5. At Key Stage 1 students are taught an awareness of character, settings, events, language, prediction, imagination and expression of personal opinions. At Key Stage 2 these are developed further by looking at the effect of language, sentence construction, different voices within the text, and themes and personal opinion supported by the text.

What the new curriculum strives for is that every student at Key Stage 1 should learn to write and read independently and with gusto. They should be able to contribute confidently orally as well as listen carefully to others. Language should represent their world as well as their imagery. Students at Key Stage 2 oracy should communicate in a way suited to purpose and audience. They should understand how language is used in fact and fiction, as well as reading a range of both and being able to respond to different layers of meaning.

The 2004/5 Ofsted Annual Report identified reasons for the varying reading attainments in primary school children. It was discovered that high standards in reading were reflective of a whole school drive towards reading. Ofsted commented that reading standards in Britain have improved over the past few years but a further intervention plan in schools is needed to continue to raise standards. Schools which rapidly covered phonics, thereby giving students the skills to decode, did better at literacy than schools that didn't; likewise schools with strong parental links did better at literacy than schools that didn't. Thus schools need to ensure that they adapt to the needs of their students. Perhaps it is worth considering children's enthusiasm and interest in television and video which could be used by schools as a powerful motivating learning tool to enhance reading and writing.

The involvement of literature in the primary arena is increasingly important. An initial introduction to literature from the child's family can help to reduce the steep learning curve that is needed with reading and literacy. Cairney (2003) maintains that shared reading with families is important in developing children's reading and writing because it is perceived as a safe environment in which to learn and make mistakes.

The hobbies of children aged between 3 and 11 are often related in some way to popular culture, television, video and computer games. Evans (2003) maintains that younger children prefer toys, yet the irony is that many toys are products of television programmes. In a survey carried out of 100 children who were asked about their out of school interests, only one replied with reading. Yet perhaps what we need to recognise, as suggested by the new national curriculum, is that children's interests and hobbies do not *exclude* literacy-related activities. Children are reading not only traditional books but screen-based texts such as computer games, websites and popular cultural texts such as comics and popular fiction. Bearne (2003a: 98) highlights that under the new national curriculum, schools need to 'approach the classroom literacy needs not only to recognise the new forms of text which children meet every day but to give multimodal texts a firm place in the curriculum'.

Heath (1983) researched the experiences of children from different cultural groups in South America. The study made comparisons between working and middle class families to investigate the varying patterns of literacy that are generated depending upon family upbringing. The research revealed that middle class children, in line with the culture of their schools, tended to have better literacy skills because their experiences of reading at home were aligned with their school reading experiences.

However, it is important to note that it is not that children brought up in working class families lack literacy skills, rather that some of them may find that their home language and literacy experience do not always fit with the literacy demands of school. Schools need to use the experiences of children's homes and communities to create a constructive learning path in schools. If we look at magazines for boys, for example, they are filled with detailed and complex texts, usually about sports or computer games. Perhaps what we should be doing, or continue to do, is not to reject the classics but to integrate them with a balance of popular mainstream reading types.

Current popular culture channels include the internet, email, texting, computer games, films and television. By using popular culture as a stimulus in early childhood, these outlets can be used to develop children's literacy skills. Fisher (2004) maintains that increasing students' desire to read must be linked with the early years of reading and trying to associate reading with play. So by making literacy more fun and cross-curricular, which I hope this book does, we can encourage children to read, write, develop their literacy skills and voice their own opinions.

Spufford (2002: 50) recalls his earliest memories of reading: 'In true fairy tales, as opposed to literary hybrids, smuggling in the techniques of the novel, there are no individual characters—only types. Good princess; bad princess ... the vocabulary of types is actually easier to acquire than knowledge about the child's own world.' Interestingly, Spufford maintains that he developed his literacy through the narrative of central characters; thus by reliving the characters in play, his literacy skills improved.

Appleyard (1990) argues that the transition of reading habits from childhood to adulthood lies in the development of thinking about a story. Curiously, a change from imagining oneself in the imaginary play world of characters to that of an analytical mindset about the characters and plot aids in the development of a child's literary skills both at home and at school.

How do we begin and continue the change process?

Literacy is an issue which all of us as teachers need to address, irrespective of the subject we teach. It is important that we understand our own reading strategy and how this compares with best practice. We need to change the way we think about teaching reading.

The new national curriculum wants to see an improvement in the progress and attainment of the literacy levels of our students. The key areas of action from the new curriculum are:

- Personalised learning (as in some of the strategies in Chapter 2).
- Assessment (as in some of the tools in Chapters 2, 3 and 4).
- The importance of literacy across the curriculum (as in Chapters 2 and 3).

Here's one I made earlier...

The importance of media literacy has become evident. The Northern Ireland Film and Television Commission/British Film Institute maintain that in order to be literate in today's society a knowledge of other text types, apart from written texts, needs to be understood and digested (NIFTC/BFI 2004). NIFTC/BFI see visual images as crucial to extending literacy.

The moving image has become a key factor in the curriculum in Northern Ireland since media awareness and its impact on children's learning has become more widespread. It is clear that children come to secondary schools armed with a wealth of literary skills, due in many cases to the years before school which are spent playing computer games, watching television and videos/DVDs. The revised curriculum in Northern Ireland reveals a new objective which aims at developing children as involved and active members of society.

The National Literacy Strategy, despite its intentions to encourage reading, seems to have brought about disaffection among young people with regards to reading (DfES 1997). Ironically, adults seem to be reading more than ever before, though still not enough. In an

Ofsted English report in 2002/3, concern was noted about media literacy not being utilised. Now it has been added to the new national curriculum in an attempt to raise literacy levels.

Vygotsky's theory of proximal development contends that children learn as a result of involvement by thinking about experience through interaction with peers or adults (Vygotsky 1962). In other words, learning occurs when external experiences become internalised. It is only when they become internalised, by identifying, comparing and categorising, that learning can be achieved. Therefore there are two levels of learning: the first is the one the child is currently demonstrating and the second is their potential—the gap between is the 'proximal zone'.

Education programmes, as discovered from my own research (Sara 2006) on children watching *Blue Peter*, can enhance learning but it is worth noting that they also need additional input to maximise learning. Children do not see films as a learning tool and therefore are more willing to absorb what is being shown—most see it as a medium for entertainment. They maintain that film watching is a tool for communication—an experience which combines learning and entertainment—and this is what results in its success. Many children are much further ahead at understanding the visual text of films than books.

So, children learn from a very young age to understand visual images. This ability varies from one child to the next due to encouragement and environment. Ironically, when children begin school there is a concern to extend verbal skills but less emphasis on visual skills.

You need support:

- From the head teacher of the school downwards.
- From your colleagues—all teachers in the school need to be in accord with language learning, regardless of specialism, as all teaching involves language and communication.
- From the children—they need to buy into this change otherwise they will become bored and disaffected.
- From parents and governors.

How are you going to implement these ideas?

Be aware of the words you use, their origin and etymology. Teach the jargon associated with specific topics and explain why we need jargon and special words.

The aim of the new national curriculum is that our students become confident and sensible young people who are able to see and understand the whole picture created by media. It wants students to recognise the vast role of media within our society, as well as developing the practical skills to use it and communicate effectively, opening up a range of opportunities both locally and globally.

After working with a group of Year 9 students studying a Shakespeare text it was evident that both visual and written texts can enhance the learning of students who are fluent and assured in literacy, as these texts together can develop critical analysis and imaginative skills. In addition, the less fluent and least assured in literacy, who tend to be reluctant readers, are drawn into the plot more readily through the use of film, which results in an increase in their engagement.

A key ingredient to reading and improving literacy skills is motivation, so the use of popular text types can encourage children to improve their literacy. Children today read *televisual text* more than any other text type. Televisual texts are a way of reading narrative. Rodriguez's 1999 study, which researched three Dominican pre-school children aged between 2½ to 5 years, looked at which texts they were drawn to at home over a nine-month period. Rodriguez discovered that the children gravitated towards screen-based text. The children were attentive viewers, especially when written text appeared on the screen. Likewise, they engaged others with the screen by actively asking questions and discussing events which had occurred.

Research carried out by Bousted and Öztürk (2004) of primary school children watching and reading *Silas Marner* revealed that students had a clearer insight into both texts than if they had only studied one. Students claimed that by studying both texts, the story 'came alive outside my head'. Perhaps what should be noted is that children come to the classroom with much insight into film usage and as teachers we must build on the different literacies that children bring with them.

Sainsbury and Schagen's 2004 research revealed that students' personal enjoyment of reading (between 1998 and 2003) has dropped considerably, to the extent that reading is no longer regarded as fun. However, students' confidence at reading has increased. The study took place over a five-year period and 5,076 students completed questionnaires about their attitudes to reading. Sainsbury and Schagen maintain that the increased confidence towards reading may be because of the use of the National Literacy Strategy. However, they claim that the reading of texts such as computers, websites, television and film have given children the opportunity to watch stories without the necessity of reading the written text, as many books have film versions and websites.

In order to increase attainment in the English curriculum active reading must be encouraged using a wide range of resources. The challenges tend to lie at the bottom and top end of ability ranges: those whose reading skills are poor and don't read, and those whose reading skills are good and yet choose not to read due to lack of commitment. In order for an effective reading culture to develop, students must be given the opportunity to explore a variety of texts in a variety of ways, alongside speaking and writing about reading.

Picture books are like films—they both invite the audience to observe. Films show a director's interpretation of the words so that the audience can come to understand through the moving image. Analysing visual images helps students to question the events taking place and thereby increases their speaking and listening skills. In addition, computer games aid in the teaching of language and literature skills as they deal with sentence-level and text-level features, such as plot, narrative construction, setting and characterisation.

It is obvious that reading and writing are keystones for the national curriculum; there is therefore a need to fuse more of the popular culture encountered at home and outside school with the needs of the classroom to help raise reading and literacy attainment. What needs to be recognised is that childhood today is very different from 20 years ago. It is more complex and traditional role models, such as those provided by family, religion and schools, do not stand so highly regarded; instead, greater emphasis is placed on popular culture.

Children profit from numerous teaching approaches in order to become good readers and writers. According to Whelehan (2002: 3), we are in the world of the image. She expresses concern about the lack of multimedia usage in schools: 'The chief problem lies in teasing out our own and others' conscious and unconscious prejudices about this kind of "hybrid" study.'

Whelehan's concern may be justified. When students lack confidence in speaking and listening it is then that images can help to clarify ideas. Movies are often the first time that children experience the culture and communication of others. My own research reveals that films enhance students' oral and written work—orally they feel more confident talking about something they have seen visually and their writing tends to encompass ideas on the screen as well as fuelling their imagination.

It seems clear that for the young this is a time of exciting change, whereas for the older generations a sense of anxiety is felt at the potential dilution of traditional print-based texts. Perhaps the problem lies in the two opposing paradigms of belief; one maintains that popular culture can be used to ignite and develop children's literacy skills, whereas the other believes that children need to be protected and shielded from technological media which have infiltrated our homes. Thus, the sooner there is an acceptance of the benefits which can be gained from different media, the sooner we can develop the reading, writing and oral skills of all students.

Images can help to clarify the meanings of words—for example, the film of a novel. Films can aid in reading provided they are chosen carefully and short clips and learning tasks are used in conjunction with them, so that clear development and characterisation can be seen. For many, multimedia texts allow students the opportunity to develop their reading and narrative analysis skills, and allow them to become absorbed in as many different text types as possible, awakening and nurturing their critical reading skills. For some students film images help illuminate the complexity of language found in some texts and therefore add to pupils' learning experiences.

The British Film Institute (2002: 5) emphasises that the moving image is a powerful global and social tool that can be used to update the knowledge of children and adults. As educators and researchers we should maximise and secure that tool within our classrooms to generate and entice further learning and develop imaginations. The BFI states: 'As the communications environment continues to change … there is little doubt that print literacy will remain a key competence, but there is also little doubt that other kinds of competence will grow in importance.'

According to the BFI, cineliteracy—the ability to draw upon a wide range of film and television literature—will eventually underpin all subjects taught in schools. In English, film can evoke discussions about narrative, characters and genres as well as increase students' confidence as readers. As for other subjects: in History, films are often used as primary sources; in Geography films allow students to gain visual insights into places and people around the world; in Art films may include animations; in Music, films provide the opportunity to embellish mood and genre through background images; in Modern Foreign Languages they offer an opportunity for students to hear and witness people in different cultures; and in Science moving image texts allow students to process knowledge more easily than still images.

It is clear that we are becoming more sophisticated as readers of visual texts, so although a group of students may watch the same film, individuals are very capable of reading the messages of the film differently. The key to interpreting the moving image is being aware that everything that you see and hear offers a message.

Story Shorts was produced by the BFI in 2001 to increase literacy at Key Stage 2, while *Screening Shorts* (2004) is aimed at aiding the teaching of literacy at Key Stage 3. The rationale behind the DVD was that most children found it easier to read a DVD than comprehend a written text. Thus the BFI felt that by marrying one with the other, attainment in children's reading and writing would improve. Specifically their aim is to increase children's ability to read visual text, setting, narrative, character, mood and genre. BFI's piloting of *Story Shorts* revealed an increase in students' levels of literacy; it was also apparent that students were motivated and found the work fun. It is clear that children absorb, interpret and analyse, albeit subconsciously, the messages of the moving image, in an attempt to make sense of what they are watching.

The impact of short films in English lessons suggests that they can be used as a scaffold for writing. Referring to film and the written text can encourage students to learn more about narrative form. It is worth noting that films are a paradox because although they offer us visual pleasure and understanding of the narrative, the visuals can sometimes differ from the words in the book. Yet just as the words on the page encourage us to read further, so does each image on the screen.

Characterisation can be developed through studying both the written text and the film version. Films give a visible picture of characters whereas the implicit descriptions of characters in written texts can remain unclear to some pupils. Genre is another construct which film can help children to understand. For example, in horror films the use of music to increase suspense and fear, the reversal of film shots, lighting and make-up all add to the power of the genre. In contrast, in a horror book the sentences would be short, the vocabulary might include scary words and lots of punctuation, and at the end of each chapter the author might use a cliff-hanger. Discussing these differences can help students to understand just how a particular genre works.

It is worth noting that novels and films differ due to the conditions of production. Some students may have the preconception that a novel is a piece of art, untainted by commercialism, whilst films are produced and packaged with the aim of box office success. However, books are promoted commercially just as vigorously as films. Perhaps the greatest hostility lies in the perceived authenticity of books to films, the latter being regarded by some as a pale reflection of the novel. However, a good film can increase the reading consumption of a text—another motivating factor worth considering.

Fundamentally, books and multimedia texts must be negotiated in order that students' attainment in English is raised. Multimedia texts are not substitutes for books but complements to the written text—and we need to encourage enthusiasm for reading and thereby literacy. To deny students a variety of texts and resources is to suppress their right to learn. The key qualities of any text are the narrative and the language, and an understanding of these can be complemented by film. After all, our contemporary culture is one in which the visual image dominates; multimedia texts and books working together can increase students' understanding of the key elements in a text.

The medium of radio should also be borne in mind as it gives students an opportunity to improve their speaking and listening skills, including clarity, tone, vocabulary, volume and articulation. It allows for information to be delivered in a structured and persuasive manner.

The written text alone is not necessarily the 'best' way of studying literature. Multimedia texts may not be popular with everyone but they are a reflection of popular reading culture today. The new national curriculum tries to create a balance between everyday text types and the traditional novel. It is by using popular culture and new media to promote literacy that we will find children's interest in reading, writing, words, speaking and listening will grow and develop.

The issues being addressed in this chapter invite us to think about literacy and the wider picture within which it falls. It is a foundation to the following chapters which aim to offer strategies to improve, or continue to improve, the literacy development of *your* students in *your* school. The practical strategies that follow present tried and tested ways to improve students' literacy, irrespective of their educational history or learning styles.

How are you going to overcome resistance?

Attitude

- All children have the ability to learn to read—as long as they are taught how to do it in accordance with the ways the brain likes to learn.

- Everyone can learn how the best methods work. Find out how you read—the chances are that most teachers were taught badly during their own schooling. You may still be using poor strategies that don't work that well. Find out what you do and how you can improve.

- Take time to talk about language in any situation. Make thinking about language interesting and fun.

- Read widely and set an example. Read fiction and non-fiction—and be prepared to talk about books, TV programmes, films, DVDs and so on which the children have access to, and about those stories which are universal themes throughout literature.

Physiology – how you sit matters

- Are you open to reading? Do you sit in an open, relaxed posture or are you trying hard to understand with your body scrunched up, your eyes screwed up, looking as though you are 'trying very hard' and yet failing?

- If you are visualising the meaning of a story, where do you see the story? Is it up in front of you somewhere? For many teachers, if you sit and look at your visual fantasies they think you are 'day-dreaming' (you are!) and think this is wrong!

When children are literate, this will not draw attention to itself—they will naturally read, naturally consult reference books, naturally sit and dream … and have a rich repertoire of stories to tell you.

Literacy is about:

- Definitions – the words we use to refer to things and experiences, understanding content and context.
- Actions – knowing how to do things, following sequences of actions to achieve intended ends.
- Values – assessing that which is better, more valuable, more interesting.
- Imagination – the creative use of language in order to experience that which has not been experienced before.

What do you want children to be able to do as a result of achieving better literacy?

- To know what words mean, and to be able to find out what words mean when they do not know; to know alternative words with similar meanings.
- To be able to explain to other people how to do things and to be able to follow instructions.
- To be able to evaluate the quality and effectiveness of all forms of communication; to be able to create particular emotional states in others through the use of language or other forms of communication.
- To be able to use language imaginatively and creatively, to be able to tell and understand stories.

The following literary skills are also useful and enable people to contribute:

- The ability to analyse the *structure* of all forms of communication in order to:
  - know how well that piece of communication works;
  - read between the lines of the communication to discover more accurately the author's intent or meaning;
  - create substantial pieces of information, literature or speech that are well-structured and able to maintain interest and entertain an audience;
  - enjoy literature, film and graphic novels at a deep level, to see and explore the connections, ramifications, the metaphors and allusions—the 'intertextuality'.

The question to ask of any piece of communication is: What do you want the other person to do as a result of understanding this message? You may not want them to do anything other than be entertained. Even so, the listener will still be busily engaged in making meaning from what you have to say. As you tell your story (in whatever form) your listeners are creating a 'shadow story' (Johnstone 1979: 79). Communication fails if the listener is not able to realise their own version of the story. This could be because there is not enough specific information or because the story doesn't hang together.

Making sense of the marks on the page

> *Alice was beginning to get very tired of sitting by her sister on the bank, and of having nothing to do: once or twice she had peeped into the book her sister was reading, but it had no pictures or conversations in it, 'and what is the use of a book,' thought Alice 'without pictures or conversation?'*

Lewis Carroll, *Alice's Adventures in Wonderland* (1865)

What the child has to learn is:

- to make sense of the squiggles and marks, and how they relate to sounds that they and other people make;
- how they join together to form words and sentences;
- how to make sense of sentences and content in terms of context;
- how what people write or say relates to what they are thinking, feeling and wanting;
- to create images and stories based on the marks which have some relationship to the author's intention.

Learning to read takes time. The probability is that young children do not have a rich enough web of associations that allow them to build 'working' images for the stories they read. There is insufficient 'geography' in the world of their imagination to allow them a sufficiently full experience which is meaningful in any way.

Therefore, during the process of being educated, each child needs to expand their working network of ways of making sense of the world. Young children are already engaged in the process of building an ever-richer web and extending their network of associations that will allow them to build working images for the stories they read. The danger is that if we don't allow time for this the child learns *not* to do it.

They need to feel successful at every stage because some aspects of decoding a text takes them out of their comfort zone and puts new demands on them—and this can be hard work, if it is treated as 'hard work'.

For example, take the second paragraph from George Eliot's *Silas Marner*, which provides a somewhat archaic way of expressing ideas:

> *In the early years of this century, such a linen-weaver, named Silas Marner, worked at his vocation in a stone cottage that stood among the nutty hedgerows near the village of Raveloe, and not far from the edge of a deserted stone-pit. The questionable sound of Silas's loom, so unlike the natural cheerful trotting of the winnowing-machine, or the simpler rhythm of the flail, had a half-fearful fascination for the Raveloe boys, who would often leave off their nutting or birds'-nesting to peep in at the window of the stone cottage, counterbalancing a certain awe at the mysterious action of the loom, by a pleasant sense of scornful superiority, drawn from the mockery of its alternating noises, along with the bent, tread-mill attitude of the weaver.*

This is not an easy passage to read and understand for a modern child. There are unfamiliar words, things which are no longer an everyday experience and the second sentence is far longer than that which is currently acceptable for clear communication. Learning to decode such a piece of writing is an acquired skill.

Here's another piece of writing which comes from *The Golden Nakara Newsletter* (November 2008):

Sixth News: The management office would like to have your participation on giving us the infor-mation of your driver and house maker who work in your place, we will bring them to file in our data base of each house and in the case that you need to have an alien staff or the one that have no ID, you will have to send the affirmation letter of responsibility and together with photo and the details information of those people to the management too.

This is not *English* English, but *Thai* English—or 'Engrish' as it is commonly known. It com-municates, but not in the way a native English person would write. Think of what we need to know about our language to be able to notice how this is different.

So what makes literacy so difficult and challenging?

Communication, when it is working, does not draw attention to itself. We only tend to notice the communication process when it's not working, when we are confused, don't understand, don't get it or do the wrong thing when following instructions.

Imagine you are putting together a self-assembly cupboard and the instructions are written in not-quite-English and has too many 'it' and gets left and right confused.

We also notice the communication process when what we want to know is not known and/or not knowable—for example, how to be an excellent writer and produce an award-winning novel, blockbuster movie script or a chart-topping pop song. Modelling an expert is not easy, and often impossible, despite what some might say—because we don't know what to pay attention to.

In speech, grammar is not usually a problem. People are able to form workable sentences and make themselves reasonably clear (see Pinker 1997). However, when it comes to formal writ-ing, the immediacy of the thought, idea or content is abandoned and the child has to engage in 'processing mode'—you have to *think about*, instead of just think. You have to switch off the 'here-and-now' and enter a kind of nowhere abstract place. And then you have to physically write or type the words, make sure they are spelled correctly, in the right sequence and with the right syntax and punctuation ... in other words, you have to attend to both content and process at the same time. No wonder you begin to fall over—you have to attend to the rules as well as the meaning.

It takes time to learn the relationship between the squiggles, the marks and the thoughts. It is possible to have perfectly constructed marks that relate to boring or meaningless ideas and thoughts; and to express great ideas in difficult to understand marks.

Teaching is usually 'upside down' in that the text—the marks—are given precedence over the ideas and thoughts that the writer is trying to express.

Chapter 2
50 Generic Strategies for Literacy Teaching

The 50 generic literacy strategies that follow cover a range of literacy issues which occur in our classrooms on a daily basis.

All of these strategies have been tried and tested and had great results. However, not all the strategies will work for all your classes. Different groups have different needs, so adapt the strategies, if need be, to the needs of your students. It is also worth noting that these strategies are only intended to be used as starters and differentiation can occur through student pairing or by using the extra resources provided for some strategies. For many of the strategies I refer to 'literacy experts'. I use this term for those students to whom you have given the role of literacy expert (because they are able to demonstrate the specific literacy skill which you are teaching to the rest of your class). For some of the strategies I have included proformas specific to that strategy.

Think of these 50 strategies as the stepping stones to a greater journey. Just take that first step with your students and watch them blossom into competent literacy users.

1 Root words

How many times have you thought to yourself, 'What is the origin of this word? Where do the parts of the word come from?' When you encounter a word new to you it is often possible to work out its meaning based on a knowledge of various morphemes, prefixes and suffixes. It is always appropriate when introducing a new word to students to take a moment to explore the meaning of the word and how it connects to other words they may know. For example, when you talk about *albumen* (the white of the egg), it can be linked to words such as *albino* (having a white, unpigmented skin), *albatross* (large white bird) or *album* (in this case, the 'white' part of the meaning of the original white sheet for writing on is no longer relevant). In the list below are some common beginnings of words which tell you something about the meaning of the word.

Root	Meaning
acou	hearing
alb	white
ante	before
anti	against
aqua	water
bi (bio-, -biotic, -be)	life
bi	two
cardi	heart
centi	hundred
chlor	green
circum	around
demi	half
ecto	outside
endo	inside
hydr	water
hyper	too much
iso	the same
macro	large
mal	bad
mega	large
micro	small
multi	many
pre	before
phot	light
sym/syn	together with
therm	heat
trans	across
uni	one
zoo	animal

- Give students the above list of root words and meanings, and ten minutes in pairs to learn the meaning of each root.
- After ten minutes, students to remove the list of root words and meanings from their sight.
- Teacher to shuffle two packs of cards. The teacher should give each student a card from the first pack of cards. The second pack of cards should be kept separate from the remainder of the first pack.
- The teacher removes a playing card from the second deck of cards and whichever student's card matches the teacher's has to answer a question about root words. An example of a question could be: What is the meaning of the root *aqua*?
- As questions about roots and meaning are answered correctly, they are displayed on the board to reinforce the meanings in students' minds.
- The game continues until all students have answered a question about which root goes with which meaning.
- If the teacher wants to continue the game, they can reverse the process and ask students which meaning goes with which root.

Cross-curricular:

- Set aside part of the lesson to introduce new subject-specific terminology.
- At the start of each topic highlight the key words.
- Display the key words for your subject on the classroom wall and give students a list—put them in the students' homework diaries.
- Run half-termly spelling bee competitions across year groups based on subject-specific terminology.

Why use this strategy?

- Root words are useful as they can help students with the spellings of many words.
- If students are able to recognise the root in a word then it will help them to work out its meaning.
- This is an effective and natural way to memorise the root meaning information.
- It motivates future learning as it helps students realise that success can be reached and can be fun.
- Paired work adds the dimension of interdependence and pair organisation—good for improving learning to learn skills.

Creativity and critical thinking - learning to learn skills:

- Developing memory
- Learning with and from others

2 Capital letters and full stops

> *Language is the dress of thought.*
> Samuel Johnson (1709–84), English author

Capital letters begin new sentences and are used for all proper nouns (e.g. days, places, months, names of people, names of buildings, organisations, institutions, periods in history, book titles, play titles, song titles). However, when they are used as adjectives capital letters are not needed.

Full stops are punctuation marks to show a strong pause. They are used at the end of a full sentence, except when the sentence is an exclamation or a question. Full stops are also used in some abbreviations, for example *e.g.*

What follows is a fun way for students to address their use of capital letters and full stops.

- Brainstorm the meaning of capital letters and full stops.
- After students have completed a piece of written work ask them to proofread their work focusing on their use of capital letters and full stops.
- After proofreading their work, ask students to decide whether their use of full stops and capital letters is OK, good or excellent. Students must be able to justify their choice.
- Now to make this strategy fun, students will transfer the OK, good or excellent comments to car types. The OK comment represents a go-kart, the good comment represents a rally car and the excellent comment represents a Formula 1 car. In order for students to progress to a car of a higher level (provided they are not at the Formula 1 level) they must improve their use of capital letters and full stops. The aim is for all students to achieve Formula 1 status. Students who achieve Formula 1 status (and this is agreed by the teacher) will be known as capital letters and full stops experts—their role will be to guide the other students' understanding of capital letters and full stops.
- The teacher asks students to pair up and explain to their partner their choice of car and how and why they reached that decision. A time limit of three minutes is given for this task.
- Afterwards, students will have to explain to the whole class the rationale for their car choice.
- The class is allowed to interject with suggestions and targets to help that student improve their use of capital letters and full stops.
- Students to fill out the 'Capital letters and full stops pit stop' proforma (see below). This will allow them to document their understanding of capital letters and full stops, as well as set targets for themselves.

Cross-curricular:

- Spend time after each piece of work getting students to check their use of full stops and capital letters.
- Display definitions of capital letters and full stops in your classroom—make students realise that it is not only the responsibility of English teachers but also for them as students.
- Give students a chart which allows them to check their use of grammar and punctuation over the course of the term (see 'Capital letters and full stops pit stop' proforma below).
- Have grammar and punctuation prefects whose responsibility it is to check that these areas are correct in students' writing.
- Print grammar and punctuation rules in homework diaries and encourage parents to help their child revise these.

Why use this strategy?

- It is essential that students are using capital letters and full stops correctly. By using this strategy, we are reinforcing the importance of capital letters and full stops in students' work at all times.
- It's fun and gets everyone involved.
- Often it is frustrating for students to have to wait for the teacher to check their classwork, so this strategy encourages students to take a more proactive approach to their own learning. Hopefully, this will encourage them to do this of their own accord.

Creativity and critical thinking – learning to learn skills:

- Developing memory
- Learning with and from others

■ Capital letters and full stops pit stop

Subject:

Term:

Which are you ... a go-kart, a rally car or a Formula 1 car?

Capital letters start a new sentence and are used for all proper nouns (e.g. days, places, months, names of people, names of buildings, organisations, institutions, periods in history, book titles, play titles, song titles). However, when they are used as adjectives no capital letters are needed.

Full stops are punctuation marks to show a strong pause. They are used at the end of a full sentence, except when the sentence is an exclamation or a question. Full stops are also used in some abbreviations, for example *e.g.*

Go-kart	Rally car	Formula 1 car
Date: *Work title:* *What puts me in this* *category?* *Target:*	*Date:* *Work title:* *What puts me in this* *category?* *Target:*	*Date:* *Work title:* *What puts me in this* *category?* *Target:*

Good luck, how quickly will you get onto the track and out of the pit stop?

3 Dictionaries

> *The greatest aim of education is not knowledge but action.*
>
> Herbert Spencer (1820–1903), English philosopher

Dictionaries are a very valuable resource for students. They can be used to look up spellings, the definition of words, capitalisation, word division and much more. The earliest known English alphabetical dictionary was written by English school teacher, Robert Cawdrey in 1604. What follows is a fun strategy which can be used to improve students' dictionary skills.

- On a table at the front of the classroom put a class set of dictionaries.
- Divide students into teams of four.
- If space permits, arrange the tables so they are at the back of the classroom. Students to sit in teams.
- At the front of the classroom, draw a goalpost on the board.
- The aim of the game is for the teacher to call out a word then each team is to write down their definition of a word and the dictionary definition of the same word. Students to fill out the 'Dictionary goal game' proforma (see below).
- The teacher calls out a word (preferably related to the subject being taught) and one student from each group has to write down what they, as a group, think the word means.
- Once that has been done, another student runs to the front, grabs a dictionary and brings it back to their group. As a team, students must look up the word and write down the dictionary definition.
- Students must then write a sentence including the word—this will check whether they can use the word in the correct context.
- After this is done, the dictionary is returned and when the group is together, they shout 'goal'. The shouting of goal is a signal for the teacher to move on to the next word.
- And so the process continues—the teacher continues to call out words and the game goes on.
- After this has happened several times, the answers are checked and the winning team puts its answer sheet into the drawn goalposts on the board.

Cross-curricular:

- Try to ensure that each table has a dictionary on it at all times so that students think they are a natural tool for learning not something that they have to request.
- Spend time after each piece of work getting students to check their spelling using a dictionary.
- Display signs which encourage students to use dictionaries.
- When reading a new text, get students to underline key words or write them down. Allow students a short amount of time to look up these words and then, as a class, share the findings.

Why use this strategy?

- Dictionaries are a valuable resource which students must be encouraged to use to check their spelling and vocabulary. This strategy encourages students' use of dictionaries.
- By making dictionary use a sports game, in this case football, it makes the process of locating definitions fun.
- It emphasises the importance of shared responsibility.
- Everyone has a role to play—it is inclusive.
- It encourages groupwork skills and thereby helps to improve students' learning to learn, provided there is a discussion about the strengths of each group and what needs to happen to improve their groupwork skills next time.
- This is a novel way to address the ongoing issue of dictionary use.

Creativity and critical thinking – learning to learn skills:

- Developing memory
- Learning with and from others

■ Dictionary goal game

Names of students in group:

Word	Our definition	Dictionary definition	Sentence

Can you achieve the accolade of top GOAL!

4 Learning and remembering spellings

> *My spelling is Wobbly. It's good spelling but it Wobbles, and the letters get in the wrong places.*
>
> A. A. Milne (1882–1956), English author

There are several techniques one can use to improve spelling. The following techniques are effective: sounds, syllables, affixes, visual memory, sight, analogy, etymology, words within words, say it, word families, mnemonics and spelling rules.

A good way to address spelling is as follows:

- Share spelling strategies with students.
- Remember to stare, conceal, note down, confirm.
- Use the spelling rules.
- Say it out loud (Mon-day).
- Look at the words inside words (conscience—con-science).
- Reduce words into sounds (r-o-o-m).
- Separate words into syllables (re-mem-ber).
- Add affixes (un+happy).
- Encourage the use of mnemonics (said—I said).
- Remember to use the same family (dissect, dissection, dissecting).
- Etymology (bi+lingual = two + languages).
- Remember to use analogy (hot, fire, cold, ice).

Using the spelling strategies just shared with the students, give out the list of words below. These words are often misspelt. Ask students to come up with strategies that might help another student who is misspelling them.

question	said	diary	where
does	because	there	February
remember	socks	liquefy	conscientious
definite	their	were	

Another good strategy is to ask pupils, as a class, to invent mnemonics for: *accommodation, medicine* and *parliament*.

When students have created the mnemonics for these words, they should share them with the class. To add to the fun factor of this strategy, the teacher should give out cards—green, yellow and red. Three students should be nominated to be the spelling experts. The first student will have the green card—this is to be held up when the answer shared with the class is correct. The second student will have the yellow card—this is held up when the answer shared is OK. The third student will have the red card—this is held up when the answer shared is wrong. Whichever expert holds up the card has to justify their card choice to the class.

Another good strategy to help students with spellings is to ask them what they understand by the phrase 'word web' (the first and the last root in each word are the starting points for a new list) and get them to complete a word web for *autograph*.

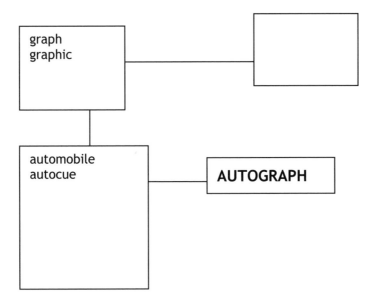

Ask students to write their own word webs for the following words: *thermometer, biology* and *democracy*. The answers should be shared with the class. Again ask the student experts to hold up the coloured cards depending on the answers given (as explained above).

Cross-curricular:

- Any subject can use these strategies and it will help students think about the meaning of words due to their similarities with other words, therefore improving spelling.
- It encourages students to use the spellcheck on computers.
- Display and give out a subject-specific vocabulary list—can this be added to school homework planners?
- Try to ensure that every classroom has subject-specific dictionaries.
- Make word and definition card boxes.
- Students create a booklet containing an alphabetical list of keywords from a unit of work. Leave a blank line alongside each. Produce a separate sheet of definitions. At the end of each lesson stress two or three keywords. Students should find those keywords in their own glossary and put the correct definitions next to each.

Why use these strategies?

- The overriding purpose of these techniques is to improve spelling—the fun factor will in most cases improve motivation and therefore learning.
- Deep learning occurs when the brain can make sense of things for itself. As the pupils will be creating a personal construct in addition to the discussion taking place, this will help cement the learning in their minds.
- Exam results will improve.

Creativity and critical thinking - learning to learn skills:

- Developing memory
- Learning with and from others
- Planning

5 Speech and quotes

...and he said and she said.

> *Speech is power: speech is to persuade, to convert, to compel.*
>
> Ralph Waldo Emerson (1803–82), American philosopher

When printing was introduced in the fifteenth century quotations were shown by referring to the speaker. This is evident in some editions of the Bible.

When using a quote, it must be put on its own line and placed within quotation marks (" "). The only time that a quote does not have to be put on its own line is if it is of three words or less.

Conversation speech follows the rules of quotes—each time a new person speaks they must have their own line. So for example:

Notice the punctuation here

"Hello," said Jonathan.

"It's a great day for a barbecue," replied Dean.

Suddenly the clouds opened and thunder and lightning attacked the grounds below.

"I guess the barbecue's off then," laughed Dean.

- Class discussion about the rules of speech and quotes.
- Students to be put into groups of four. Each group has four roles—two actors, one narrator and one literacy expert. Students to decide who is to take on which role.
- Students to write a script between two well-known people from that subject (e.g. Jenson Button and Lewis Hamilton, Flintoff and Pieterson, Einstein and Currie, Shakespeare and Sara!) or two students who are discussing the key points of the topic being studied.
- The written speech is to last no longer than three minutes. The two actors will act, the narrator will narrate (e.g. as the characters speak, the narrator adds in their voice: *He said*, *She laughed* and so on) and the literacy expert will interject explaining where the speech and quotes go as the performance occurs.
- The aim of the task is twofold—firstly, to impart knowledge to the rest of the class about the topic at hand and secondly, to highlight how speech and quotes are laid out in the written text.

Cross-curricular:

- Begin the lesson by asking your literacy expert to explain the rules of speech and quotes.
- This is a good revision tool for all topic areas.
- Remember to display the rules of speech and quotes on your classroom wall.
- Put copies of speech and quote rules in students' homework diaries.

Why use this strategy?

- The purpose of this strategy is to reinforce the grammatical rules of speech and quotes.
- It's a fun way to strengthen these rules which have been learnt already in English lessons.
- It encourages teamwork and develops groupwork skills—it is therefore excellent for developing learning to learn.
- This is a creative and kinaesthetic activity—it will suit these learners in particular.
- As this is a drama-based activity it will allow some students easier access to the curriculum.
- It's inclusive, so everyone will be involved.

Creativity and critical thinking – learning to learn skills:

- Developing memory
- Learning with and from others
- Planning
- Thinking

6 Homophones

Reading in Reading!

> *The wisest mind has something yet to learn.*
>
> George Santayana (1863–1952), Spanish philosopher

Homophones are words that sound the same when spoken but are spelt differently and have a different meaning (e.g. peace, piece). The Greek prefix *homo* means 'the same'.

Some other examples of homophones are:

there, their, they're
whether, weather
allowed, aloud
pear, pair

What follows is a fun strategy to address students' use of homophones.

- Give students a list of homophones (see list below—this is not exhaustive, please add to it).
- Class discussion about homophones.
- Teacher to display around the room various fuel types—unleaded petrol, diesel, LPG, biofuel, electricity, hybrids, solar power, hydrogen.
- In pairs, students to walk around the room and read about the fuel varieties. For the benefit of this exercise, the fuel varieties will be classed as: basic (unleaded petrol, diesel), advanced (LPG, biofuel, electricity) and premium (hybrids, solar power, hydrogen).
- Now to make this strategy fun, students will transfer their accuracy with homophones to fuel types. So students who are OK with their use of homophones can choose between unleaded petrol or diesel. Students who show a good understanding of homophones can choose between LPG, biofuel or electricity. Students who show excellent use of homophones can choose between hybrids, solar power or hydrogen. In order for students to progress to a fuel of a higher level (provided they are not at the premium level) they must improve their use of homophones. The aim is for all students to achieve premium fuel status. Students who achieve premium fuel status (and this is agreed by the teacher) will be known as the homophones experts. Their role will be to guide the other students in their understanding of homophones.
- Students to work in pairs. Students are given a time limit to write a sentence for each of the homophones on the initial list.
- Once the time limit is up, pairs swap answers with another pair.
- In order to achieve basic fuel status, students must get 14 correct homophones—otherwise their driving licence will be revoked! Sixteen correct homophones allows students to upgrade to an advanced fuel type and 22 correct homophones allows students to upgrade to a premier fuel type.
- Class discussion to clarify results is held and fuel rankings issued.
- Teacher to ensure students record their ranking so that they can continue from this fuel ranking point next time the teacher chooses to play the game.

Cross-curricular:

- Display homophones on the classroom wall and refer and point to them regularly.
- Remember to run half-termly vocabulary competitions across year groups.
- Print homophone lists in homework diaries and encourage parents to help their child learn these words.
- If resources permit, keep dictionaries and thesauruses on desks and encourage students to use them. I've found that students will use them more willingly if they are in front of them, rather than if they have to ask.
- Have a homophone of the week—encourage students to use it correctly.
- Have a homophone expert whose responsibility is to ensure that students are learning new homophones and using them correctly.
- This game can be continued in other subjects—students can carry over their fuel ranking points, provided it has been written in diaries and signed by staff!

Why use this strategy?

- Learning the correct use of homophones is vital if students are to do well and excel.
- It's a fun strategy and should motivate students to learn.
- There is an inclusive feel to the game, so everyone has to take responsibility for their learning.
- It suits the kinaesthetic learner who likes to be active!

Creativity and critical thinking – learning to learn skills:

- Developing memory
- Learning with and from others
- Planning
- Thinking
- Investigating resources

■ List of most commonly confused homophones

there, their, they're	one, won	here, hear
where, were, wear	to, too, two	bored, board
our, are	which, witch	see, sea
piece, peace	whole, hole	week, weak
whether, weather	would, wood	plain, plan
allowed, aloud	through, threw	saw, sore
pear, pair	write, right	
caught, court	heal, heel	

■ Fuel car choices

Unleaded Petrol

This is the most popular fuel with UK motorists. It's quieter than diesel, and if you have a problem with your engine it is cheaper to repair. It works quite well! However, it's the least environmentally friendly, is non-renewable and produces most CO_2.

Diesel

This is growing in popularity because it has lower CO_2 emissions and is therefore more environmentally friendly. However, it is loud and the ride is less smooth.

Liquid Petroleum Gas (LPG)

This is also known as autogas. LPG is cheaper than petrol and it is easy to convert your car to autogas as it omits fewer emissions than diesel and petrol and is less noisy than diesel. The only problem is that LPG is not available at every garage. Overall, it is good for saving money and the environment.

Biofuels

Biofuels power cars by using renewable energy sources. Biofuels can be difficult to find for the environmentally conscious driver but have low CO_2 emissions and offer high performance!

Electricity

The great thing about these cars is that they can be charged in garages or at home! You won't have to pay car tax or congestion charge if you live in London. However, they do need a lot, and I mean a lot, of electricity! Often they do not run for more than 50 miles and they tend to have a top speed of 40-50 mph!

Hybrids

Hybrids are a mix of a rechargeable electric system and a fuel-based engine. They tend to consume less fuel but the problem is that they are expensive and not as effective as high performance cars. Cool!

Hydrogen

Hydrogen vehicles are very environmentally friendly—they give off no bad emissions! However, hydrogen is very, very flammable! But super-cool!

Solar power

OK, so we don't see many of these and they look like spaceships but like hydrogen cars they are very environmentally friendly—they give off no emissions! They are however not very effective if you live in a cloudy or rainy country and not good for night-time driving as they are charged through solar panels! But very eco-friendly and super-cool!

7 Connectives – How far can you run?

> *Words are the only things that last forever.*
>
> **William Hazlitt (1778–1830), English writer**

Connectives are used to link two clauses or sentences. Some examples of connectives are: *also, and, too, furthermore* and *moreover*.

The following is an effective strategy to encourage students to use connectives correctly.

- Class discussion about connectives (see 'Examples of connectives' below).
- Clear the desks and chairs to the side of the room—this activity would benefit from a large space.
- Put students in four (or more if need be) running teams.
- The aim of the game is to see which team has the greatest understanding of connectives. Now to make this strategy fun, students' understanding of connectives will be related to running. So, which team can run the furthest (i.e. which team knows the most about connectives)?

  Is your team a 5 km?
  Is your team a 10 km?
  Is your team a half-marathon?
  Is your team running for the London Marathon?

  In front of each team are 26 sheets of paper—each paper denotes 1 km.

- Teacher or student expert to ask questions about the correct use of connectives basing the question in subject-specific knowledge.
- Each team is to answer one question and if they get the question right the first player goes on to the 1 km paper and if they can identify the connective in the question, they can progress to the 2 km paper.
- The next team plays—if they can't answer the question, or can't answer it correctly, the question goes to the first team which shouts 'connectives'. If that team answers correctly it means that one of their team can go straight to the London Marathon—provided they have not set foot on the 1 km paper yet.
- And so the game continues, until one whole team has made it to the London Marathon.
- Alternatively, immediate 'passes' to the London Marathon are available to any players who have not made the 1 km sheet if they can give two facts about the chosen subject using connectives correctly.

Cross-curricular:

- At the start of each topic allow a couple of students to be known as the experts of that literacy area—they are to ensure that all students are up to speed with the specific literacy skills being developed. At the start of the lesson allow your experts to reintroduce connectives.

- Display connectives on your classroom wall (see 'Examples of connectives' proforma below) and give students a connective list—put them in the students' homework diaries.
- Give out connective sheets to those students who would benefit. It might be worthwhile getting students to write down facts about the subject being addressed using connectives in case they have the opportunity to ask for a 'pass'.
- Look at a video clip of a running race and interject with statements about the race using connectives. Model a short piece of writing which uses connectives to explain the race.

Why use this strategy?

- It encourages students to use connectives!
- It encourages teamwork and develops groupwork skills—it is therefore excellent for learning to learn.
- It suits learners who like to be active.
- It's fun and allows students to test out their understanding of different literacy definitions.
- It's a good way of revising literacy skills across the curriculum.
- Drama can allow some students easier access to the curriculum.

Creativity and critical thinking – learning to learn skills:

- Learning with and from others
- Thinking

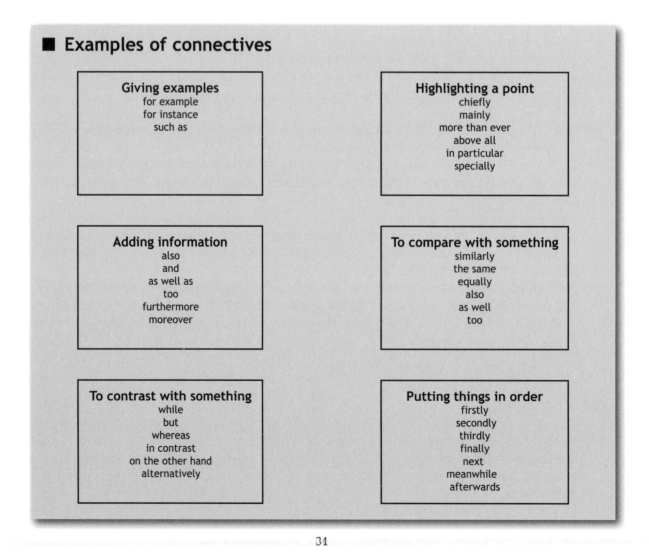

■ Examples of connectives

Giving examples
for example
for instance
such as

Highlighting a point
chiefly
mainly
more than ever
above all
in particular
specially

Adding information
also
and
as well as
too
furthermore
moreover

To compare with something
similarly
the same
equally
also
as well
too

To contrast with something
while
but
whereas
in contrast
on the other hand
alternatively

Putting things in order
firstly
secondly
thirdly
finally
next
meanwhile
afterwards

8 Vocabulary size

> *One forgets words as one forgets names. One's vocabulary needs constant fertilising or it will die.*
>
> Evelyn Waugh (1903–66), English writer

'No dear, don't use the word nice—be more adventurous.'

'But Miss said …'

'Not said dear, please try to be more adventurous with your word choices!'

Widening our vocabulary size as students is the same as upgrading our car as adults—or so it should be. Vocabulary usually expands with age and is an essential tool in communicating. What follows is an effective strategy to extend students' vocabulary.

- Teacher to write three different vocabulary lists and give them to students.
- Teacher to tell students that the first list has the basic words needed for that subject—it is known as the Basic Cars list. The second list contains more advanced vocabulary—it is known as the Saloon Car list. The third list includes the advanced vocabulary—it is known as the Super Car list.
- Students to be given the blank 'Vocabulary list' proforma (see below). Teacher to highlight that each car category has three cars which fit under that heading. Students to choose a car from each section that they aspire to own:
  - Basic Cars: Smart, Skoda, Fiat
  - Saloon Cars: Volkswagen, Volvo, Saab
  - Super Cars: Pagani Zonda, Lamborghini, Ferrari
- The aim is for students to be able to explain the vocabulary in the basic car list and their meanings. Once this has been done they can progress to the next car level and therefore the next vocabulary list.
- At the start of each lesson, or once a week, students to be given ten minutes to revise the words and meanings of whichever car they aspire to (provided they have achieved the lower class cars).
- After ten minutes, the teacher chooses a car type and tests those students on their vocabulary list.
- The test could ask students to match up a word with a similar longer word from their vocabulary list and use it in a sentence.
- Once a student has Super Car status, then their role changes and they become an expert. Their role is to help other students increase their vocabulary as well as creating a new higher level list called Formula 1.

Cross-curricular:

- Spend time introducing new subject-specific terminology.
- Display key words on the classroom wall and refer and point to them regularly.
- Display the key words for your subject on the wall.
- Run half-termly vocabulary competitions across year groups based on subject-specific terminology.
- Print vocabulary lists in homework diaries and encourage parents to help their child learn these words.
- Keep dictionaries on desks and encourage students to use them. Students will use them more willingly if they are in front of them rather than if they have to ask.
- Have a school 'word of the week' that all teachers and form tutors try to encourage students to use correctly and in context. This word should be displayed in all classrooms and on the student intranet.

Why use this strategy?

- Learning new vocabulary is vital if students are to do well and excel in subjects.
- It's fun and it motivates students to learn as they realise they can succeed.
- This will increase students' natural instincts to learn new words if it is being given such a high focus.

Creativity and critical thinking – learning to learn skills:

- Learning with and from others
- Thinking
- Investigating resources

■ Vocabulary list

Subject:

Term:

Basic Car choice:

Saloon Car choice:

Super Car choice:

BASIC CAR:	SALOON CAR:	SUPER CAR:
Smart	Volkswagen	Pagani Zonda
Skoda	Volvo	Lamborghini
Fiat	Saab	Ferrari

Good luck, how quickly will you get to pole position?

9 Thesauruses

> *Learning is not attained by chance, it must be sought for with ardour and attended to with diligence.*
>
> **Abigail Adams (1744–1818), wife of John Adams, the second President of the USA**

Thesauruses, like dictionaries, are valuable resources for students. Thesauruses contain synonyms and antonyms. The word *thesaurus* comes from the ancient Greek and means 'storehouse' or 'treasury'. What follows is an effective technique which addresses students' use of thesauruses.

- Put students into groups of four.
- The aim of the game is very similar to the 'football goal' dictionary game (see Strategy 3). Firstly, each team is to write down what they think is an alternative word for the word the teacher calls out, and secondly, each team must write down the dictionary definition of that word.
- On a table at the front of the classroom put a class set of thesauruses.
- If space permits, arrange the tables at the back of the classroom. Students to sit in teams.
- At the front of the classroom, draw rugby posts on the board. Each group given a 'Thesaurus try game' proforma (see below).
- The teacher calls out a word (preferably related to that subject) and each group has to write an alternative similar word on the proforma. Once that has been done, one student from each group runs to the front, grabs a thesaurus and dictionary and brings it back to their group. As a group they look up the word in the thesaurus, choose one of the suggestions (preferably their original choice if it is there) and write it down on the proforma. Then using the dictionary they write up the meaning of the word.
- Students write on the proforma a sentence using the chosen word correctly.
- The thesaurus is returned and when the group is together they shout 'Try'. Brief class discussion about word and sentence choice.
- And so the process continues, each time trying to speed up the process.
- After this has happened several times the answers are checked and the winning team puts its answer sheet into the drawn rugby posts on the board.

Cross-curricular:

- Spend time after each piece of work getting students to improve their vocabulary choices with a thesaurus.
- Ensure that each table has a dictionary and thesaurus on it at all times so that students think they are a natural tool for learning not something that they have to request.
- Display signs which encourage students to use a thesaurus.
- When reading a text, get students to suggest alternative similar words that can be interchanged with words in the text.

Why use this strategy?

- It reminds students why we should use a thesaurus.
- By basing thesaurus use on a sports game, in this case rugby, it makes thesauruses more fun.
- It emphasises the importance of sharing responsibility.
- Everyone has a role to play—it is inclusive.
- It encourages groupwork skills and thereby helps to improve students' learning to learn, provided there is a discussion about the strengths of each group and what needs to happen to improve groupwork skills next time.
- This is a novel way to address the ongoing issue of thesaurus use.

Creativity and critical thinking – learning to learn skills:

- Learning with and from others
- Thinking
- Investigating resources

■ Thesaurus try game

Names of students in group:

Word	Our alternative word choice	Thesaurus word selection	Dictionary meaning	Word chosen in a sentence

Can you achieve the accolade of top TRY!

10 Paragraphs

Organising is what you do before you do something, so that when you do it, it is not all mixed up.

A. A. Milne (1882–1956), English author

Paragraphs are needed in all subjects. Paragraphs should divide work into topics. Each paragraph should discuss one key point, so that the reader is able to state what each paragraph is about. The topic sentence should be a signpost directing the reader through the writing.

- Teacher-led discussion about paragraphs and indenting.
- One essay is cut up into paragraphs. The key points from each paragraph are written onto separate pieces of paper and placed randomly around the room on the wall.
- Teacher tells students the essay title.
- Students in mixed ability groups of three gather the key points for each paragraph of the essay title and then decide upon the order for the structure of the essay.
- In groups, students to write the main points that go with each paragraph and then transfer those points into sentences.
- Additional table of resources available for those students who are less able—on the table are the actual cut out paragraphs from the model essay and the less able students will need to place them in the correct order.
- Students may use the teacher as a resource to get feedback about their progress.
- As a group, students write the essay (preferably on computers, using the spellcheck) and then share with the class. Time limit given.
- Class discussion about the strengths and areas to develop of each group's paragraph choices.
- Hand out 'Paragraphs pit stop' proforma (see below). Now to make this strategy fun, students will transfer their ability to use paragraphs correctly by comparing themselves to car types. So if they are a basic user of paragraphs then they must complete their comments in the go-kart column, if they are a good user of paragraphs then they must complete their comments in the rally car column and if they are an excellent user of paragraphs then they must complete their comments in the Formula 1 car column. In order for students to progress to a car of a higher level (provided they are not at the Formula 1 level) they must improve their use of paragraphs. The aim is for all students to achieve Formula 1 status. Students who achieve Formula 1 status (and this is agreed by the teacher) will be known as the paragraph experts—their role will be to guide the other students' understanding of paragraphs.
- Students to fill out proforma. This will allow them to document their understanding of paragraphs, as well as set targets for them to improve.

Cross-curricular:

- Spend time after each piece of work getting students to check their use of paragraphs.
- Use your grammar and punctuation experts whose responsibility it is to check that these areas are OK in students' writing.
- Print paragraph rules in homework diaries and encourage parents to help their child revise these.

Why use this strategy?

- It reminds students to use paragraphs correctly.
- It allows students to work with each other and develop their groupwork skills.
- As there is a fun element to this task, it should help to develop relaxed relationships in the class.
- It gets all students involved—it's inclusive and feels like a game as the students are competing against the clock.
- The moving around the room element keeps students alert as it has a kinaesthetic element.
- Once the task is complete it is important to focus on the learning to learn skills the students have used—and what they need to develop to become better learners.

Creativity and critical thinking - learning to learn skills:

- Learning with and from others
- Planning
- Thinking
- Investigating resources

■ Paragraphs pit stop

Subject:

Term:

Paragraphs divide your work into topics. Each paragraph should discuss one key point, so that the reader is able to state what each paragraph is about. The topic sentence should be a signpost directing the reader through the writing.

Go-kart	Rally car	Formula 1 car
Date: *Work title:* *What puts me in this category?* *Target:*	*Date:* *Work title:* *What puts me in this category?* *Target:*	*Date:* *Work title:* *What puts me in this category?* *Target:*

Good luck, how quickly will you get onto the track and out of the pit stop?

11 Apostrophe snap!

Only in grammar can you be more than perfect.
William Safire (1929–), American author

There are two types of apostrophe—omission and possession.

Let's revise *omissions*:

> It's – it is
> You've – you have
> Don't – do not
> Isn't – is not

… and so on, so two words combine to become one.

OK, so now *possessive apostrophes*:

We use these to show that one thing belongs to another. For example:

Einstein's Bunsen burner. We see from the use of the possessive apostrophe that the Bunsen burner belonged to Einstein.

Jenny's dad was late picking her up from the maths quiz. The addition of *'s* to Jenny shows the reader that it was her dad who was late.

Foreign words, especially in Arabic and Japanese, use apostrophes to divide and distance syllables and letters, otherwise it is thought they would be incorrectly interpreted. In science fiction, alien names have apostrophes—often this is for decoration.

The following is a strategy which can be used to improve students' use of apostrophes.

- Teacher brainstorms apostrophes with the whole class.
- The teacher tells the class they will play 'Apostrophe snap!'—a game similar to the card game snap.
- Teacher gives out several blank cards (playing card size) to students.
- In pairs students write five questions and five answers about the topic being studied at present on the cards. Students write questions on one card and answers on another card.
- The only rule is that each question card has to contain an apostrophe.
- Two pairs join together and each pair works as a team to win against the other pair in answering the questions correctly. Students have to answer the questions correctly and explain where the apostrophe sits in the question asked.
- The scoring is as follows—one mark awarded for every correct apostrophe stated and one mark awarded for every four correct facts answered about the topic.
- When all questions have been asked, the game is over. The pair in each team with the highest score shout 'Apostrophe snap!'

Cross-curricular:

- When checking through work get students to hold up apostrophe cards to show that they recognise that an apostrophe is necessary.
- Add apostrophe rules to students' homework diaries.
- Display apostrophe rules in your classroom and refer to them.
- Promote a student to apostrophe expert. Their role is to ensure the rest of the class is up to speed using apostrophes correctly. At the start of the lesson allow your experts to reintroduce literacy subject-specific terminology.
- This is a good revision tool for all subjects and it can also be used for testing other literacy skills, not just apostrophes.

Why use this strategy?

- It is important that students use apostrophes correctly and this strategy emphasises the importance without the blandness of a straightforward grammar lesson. Also, the more cross-curricular literacy that takes place, the more likely students will develop these skills of their own accord.
- It encourages a competitive element within students which will hopefully make them master the use of apostrophes.
- It encourages teamwork and develops groupwork skills—it is therefore excellent for learning to learn.
- It is fun.
- It's a good way of revising topics as well as reinforcing the rules of apostrophes.

Creativity and critical thinking – learning to learn skills:

- Learning with and from others
- Thinking

12 Proofreading

> *Law is order, and good law is good order.*
> Aristotle (384–322 BC), Greek philosopher

Proofreading gives us all a chance to ensure that we do not have any mistakes in our work. It does not matter how young or old we are, we all make grammatical errors. We all try to visit the dentist for check-ups and if we drive we take our car for a service. Proofreading is the same. It's another check-up—something that needs to be done to make sure our work runs smoothly across the lines of the page.

- Put students into teams of four.
- Students to proofread each others' completed written task.
- Each student in the team is given a title. The titles are taken from the roles in cricket—bowler, umpire and two batsmen.
- The aim for each team is to score the most against the other batting teams in the room (i.e. to have the best proofread work) having gained maximum marks on the proofreading proforma (see below).
- For each group, the definition of the roles is as follows: the bowler ensures that the categories on the list below are addressed; the umpire ensures that everyone is on task, the objectives of the game are being met and any resources needed are being used, e.g. dictionaries; and the batsmen are responsible for proofreading the text and making suggested changes as a result of the proofreading.
- The game begins. All teams are allowed one opportunity to ask the teacher for advice.
- To vary the activity, work can be rotated around the room with the proofread sheet being checked by the other teams.
- When the time is up, draw the class together and discuss what the common errors in students' work are, what targets can be set and what learning to learn skills we must develop to make this task even better.

Cross-curricular:

- If work is on computer, try to get a hard copy as it is easier to spot mistakes on paper than on a computer screen.
- Remember to get students to use the spellcheck or a dictionary when checking work.
- Common mistakes tend to be: incorrect use of homophones, incorrect use of endings or suffixes, leaving out letters in a word, missing out words, mistakes with subject–verb agreement, i before e rule, apostrophes, using one word when you should use two and using a small i as a pronoun.
- Spend time after each piece of work getting students to check their work.
- Display signs which encourage students to proofread.

Why use this strategy?

- Proofreading is an essential skill. This strategy encourages proofreading in a fun and safe environment.
- Basing proofreading on a sports game, in this case cricket, makes it fun.
- The game is inclusive and everyone has a role to play, so everyone gets involved.
- This game encourages the development of groupwork skills.
- This is a novel way to address the ongoing issue of proofreading.
- It requires students to be critical of work in a constructive manner which will hopefully rub off onto their way of judging their own work.
- It highlights the importance of joint responsibility.

Creativity and critical thinking – learning to learn skills:

- Learning with and from others
- Planning
- Thinking

■ Proofreading

Have I checked the following?

	Have I checked? (✓ or ✗)	I need to check what this is? (✓ or ✗)	Notes to help me remember what this is …
Use of capital letters and full stops			
Use of paragraphs			
Have I used the correct homophones?			
Have I used the correct ending/suffix?			
I have used the correct subject-verb agreement?			
Have I remembered the i before e rule?			
Have I used apostrophes correctly?			
Have I used one word when I should have used two?			
Are my facts correct?			
Have I answered the question?			
Does it make sense?			
Have I proofread my work?			
Has my friend proofread my work?			

13 Herringbone Pattern

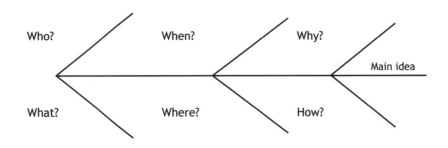

It is not true we have only one life to love; if we can read, we can live as many lives and as many kinds of lives as we wish.

Samuel I. Hayakawa (1906–92), Canadian born academic and political figure

The Herringbone Pattern (Walker 2000) is best used after the initial reading or skimming of a section of work in order to remember the key points. The Herringbone Pattern helps students to understand the information they are reading by allowing them to put it in a fun and easy format.

Pupils are given a time limit to read a section of, for example, a chapter. Afterwards, they fill in the Herringbone Pattern: What is the main point of the chapter? Who is the narrator? When, what and how has it occurred? Why? Pupils write short sentences answering these questions on the diagonal lines by each question. In the centre of the Herringbone Pattern is the 'main idea', which is what the pupils should refer back to.

- Get everyone to draw the Herringbone Pattern.
- Get students to label the pattern with the key words—Who? What? When? Where? Why? How?
- Give students a short amount of time to read a text and then in pairs ask everyone to fill out the answers to the questions in the Herringbone Pattern.
- The first student to finish shouts 'Herringbone'. They should feed back their answers to the whole class. As the student is reading out their answers, other students tick any matching or similar responses. If, however, the class feel that the answer given by the student is incorrect, they should shout out 'Herringbone Pattern' and explain their opinion.

Cross-curricular:

- Ideal for revising topics.
- It's a good way to assess prior knowledge—a good starter.
- It's a good plenary to check understanding.

Why use this strategy?

- It's fun for both the teacher and students!
- It allows the teacher to see how much everyone has understood from the text.

Creativity and critical thinking – learning to learn skills:

- Planning
- Thinking

14 Sentences

It is essential that students can recognise a good and a bad sentence. In order to do so, they must be familiar with the key ingredients: noun, verb, adverb and possessive pronoun.

e.g. Their cat meows loudly.

- As a class discuss the key ingredients needed for a perfect sentence.
- Students to be in groups of four.
- Each group is given four envelopes which contain a list of words—one envelope consists mostly of nouns, one of verbs, one of possessive pronouns and one of adverbs.
- Teacher to explain that in their groups the students should make the perfect sentence.
- The aim of the task is for each group to make complete sentences using all the words from the envelopes.
- If a group completes the task accurately, according to the teacher, these group members are disbanded and they become the sentence experts and are to help other groups.

Cross-curricular:

- Irrespective of the subject, students need to write sentences correctly.
- This game can be made up of facts from a particular subject. To make the game subject-specific, the words in the envelopes could be facts about the topic being studied at present.
- At the start of each topic, allow a couple of students to be known as the experts of the literacy area. Their role is to ensure that all students are up to speed with the specific literacy skills being developed.
- Remember to display information on your classroom walls about how to write a correct sentence.

Why use this strategy?

- It is vital that students can construct sentences correctly and this is a good way of reinforcing the rules of sentences.
- It encourages teamwork and develops groupwork skills—it is therefore excellent for learning to learn.
- It's fun.
- It's a good way to revise cross-curricular literacy.
- It's a good way to revise a topic.

Creativity and critical thinking – learning to learn skills:

- Learning with and from others
- Thinking
- Investigating resources

15 Make me an author! Are you an author or an editor?

> *There is more treasure in books than in all the pirate's loot on Treasure Island.*
>
> Walt Disney (1901–66), Academy award-winning US film producer

It is important that when reading all students are attentive and absorb the information being imparted. What follows is a strategy which will help students' reading skills.

- Class discussion about strategies needed when reading a text: drawing upon prior knowledge (e.g. any other knowledge about the plot, author, context); understanding what the purpose of the text is; ability to decode words (think about root words); continually checking understanding and visualising images in your head and sharing those images with your neighbour; making predictions; ability to ask questions; ability to summarise the text; applying what you have learnt to what is being asked of you.
- All students to be given the same piece of text to read. In pairs, students read the text.
- After the text has been read, each pair must decide who will take on the acting role of the author of the text and who will take on the role of the editor of the text.
- In pairs, pupils to complete the 'Make me an author! Are you author or editor?' proforma (see below). The editor will ask the author the questions on the sheet. However, they will need to work together to decide upon the answers which will be based on the text they have just read.
- This is a race to see which team (or publishing house) can answer the points correctly and in detail.
- As soon as a team has all the answers then the teacher is to stop the teams and a class discussion about the answers occurs.

Cross-curricular:

- The great thing about this activity is that you can adapt it for any subject—you just need to find a text related to your subject area.
- You could list famous authors from your subject and put them on the board with pictures or video clips so that students can relate to subject-specific authors.
- This is a great way to assess learning at the end of a topic or lesson.

Why use this strategy?

- No matter which subject students study they will need to be able to respond to written text, so this is beneficial to every subject.
- This activity encourages students to be more aware of the skills needed when reading a text.
- Although this is a serious strategy which students need to be aware of, the context in which it is done—Are you an author or an editor?—gives it a fun element.
- It reinforces the idea that to learn effectively we need to ask questions and analyse texts.
- It encourages students to work effectively in pairs and thereby promotes learning to learn.

Creativity and critical thinking – learning to learn skills:

- Learning with and from others
- Planning
- Thinking
- Investigating resources

■ Make me an author! Are you author or editor?

Names of pairs and roles:
1.   2.

Title of text:

Topic:

1. What prior knowledge do you have about the subject you are reading (comment on author, context, time written, similar plots)?

2. What is the purpose of what you are reading?

3. Words you need to decode—write down the word and meaning (use a dictionary).

4. Are you checking your understanding of what you have learnt? How are you doing that?

5. Are you visualising the images inside your head? What are you seeing?

6. Are you making predictions? What are those predictions?

7. Are you asking questions? What questions have you asked?

8. Can you summarise the text? Write your summary here.

9. What have you learnt and what is being asked of you?

So who is the real author and who is the real editor?

16 Notes

> *A book is a garden carried in the pocket.*
> Chinese proverb

Note taking is good skill to use when reading. It is an important skill, which allows us to put large quantities of information quickly on the page. Various methods can be used: diagrams, mind maps, spider diagrams, flow charts, copying, key words, Post-its, highlighting, underlining and writing key points in the margin of a book.

- Class discussion about note taking techniques and why we take notes.
- All students to be given the same text.
- In pairs, students to make notes on the text using one of the techniques above.
- Time limit given.
- Teacher collects in original texts.
- Each pair, using their notes, explains to the class the content of the text.
- Discussion about whose notes are best and why.

Cross-curricular:

- The text given out can be about a topic you are studying at present.
- At the start of each topic, allow a couple of students to be known as the experts of the literacy area. Their role is to ensure that all students are up to speed with the specific literacy skills being developed.
- Remember to display information on your classroom walls about how to make notes.

Why use this strategy?

- It is vital that students can make notes as they will need them for many aspects of their studying.
- It encourages teamwork and develops groupwork skills—it is it is therefore excellent for learning to learn.
- It's fun.
- It's a good way to revise cross-curricular literacy.
- It's a good way to revise a topic.

Creativity and critical thinking – learning to learn skills:

- Learning with and from others

17 Past, present and future questions

> *The important thing is not to stop questioning.*
>
> **Albert Einstein (1879–1955), German-born physicist**

- Put several resources (books, photocopies of texts, artefacts, computers for internet research) about one topic on a table.
- Teacher to introduce the topic and give out 'Past, present and future questions' proforma (see below).
- Students in pairs to fill in the proforma which asks them about their present knowledge of the topic and what they hope to know by the end of the lesson. The proforma should awaken students to past and new knowledge about what they have learnt and what they want to learn.
- Class discussion about points written on the proforma.
- Students in pairs make notes about the topic being researched using the resources on the table to help them. Students should be given a time limit to do this.
- Once the time is up, students return to their desks.
- Teacher-led discussion about the 'process' and how this strategy has helped them.
- Students complete the other two columns of the proforma.

Cross-curricular:

- This strategy is suitable for any subject.
- This strategy is especially useful as a reading strategy.
- It clarifies in the readers' minds what they already know.
- Students can do this is pairs. Paired work will mean that students can bounce ideas off each other and share their joys and concerns—so they know they are not alone!
- Remember to display this strategy on the wall and visually refer to it.
- Have a copy of this strategy within the students' homework diaries.

Why use this strategy?

- This strategy is a useful reading strategy because it gets students thinking about past, present and future knowledge—what they want to learn.
- The strategy tends to boost students' confidence because by the end they have written down what they learnt during the lesson—and writing down your own achievements tends to boost your self-confidence.
- It helps to clarify students' prior knowledge in order that they know where they are going.
- It encourages teamwork and develops groupwork skills—it is therefore excellent for learning to learn.
- It's a good way of revising a topic, as well as developing a strategy to approach reading.

Creativity and critical thinking – learning to learn skills:

- Learning with and from others
- Planning
- Investigating resources

■ Past, present and future questions

PAST: My knowledge about this topic at the moment *Write down three questions which you would like answered by the end of the lesson*	FUTURE: My hopes for my knowledge at the end of this lesson	PRESENT: My knowledge at the end of the lesson	QUESTIONS I NOW HAVE:

Information learnt:

18 Prediction

Prediction is a useful tool for students to use to develop their reading skills. It requires students to look for clues in the text to guess and logically work out what will happen next.

- Introduce prediction and the skills needed (see 'Prediction chart' proforma below).
- Put students into groups of four and tell them they will need to take on the role of detectives.
- As a class revise the role of a detective. The detectives read a text together, locate the clues in the text, predict and solve what will happen next for their police report.
- Firstly, the teacher is to give each group a scenario from which they are to predict the outcome. Students are also given the proforma to complete.
- Students are then given another clue—a piece of subject-specific text to help them with their predictions. Based upon that text, they are to refine their predictions.
- Teacher to read out the actual prediction. How many groups got it right?
- During the game, students can ask for a clue from the teacher. If a clue is asked for, the teacher will give them an object which will help them with their prediction. Groups can only ask for one clue per game.
- It is important to have a discussion at the end of the activity about the steps taken by the students when using predictions and what makes some predictions successful and others not.

Cross-curricular:

- This is a good strategy for all subjects—at some point students have to read and respond to written material.
- In English staff can use it to ask students to predict stories.
- In History this works well as you can ask students to predict the outcomes of historical events.
- In Science students can predict the results of experiments based on their initial reading.
- Prediction is an important life skill as it is useful when making life decisions.

Why use this strategy?

- We want students to predict whilst reading—this strategy reinforces student self-belief that they can do this.
- It stimulates students and is fun!
- It reminds students of the importance of scratching below the surface to find the truth.
- It's inclusive as everyone has to contribute to solve the prediction.
- It requires students to be critical of other students' work in a constructive manner, which will hopefully encourage students to be critical of their own work.

- It highlights the importance of working together as a team to locate the clues—joint responsibility.

Creativity and critical thinking – learning to learn skills:

- Learning with and from others
- Planning
- Thinking

■ **Use the prediction chart to help you work out what will happen next**

➤ What has happened?

➤ Who is involved?

➤ Where has this happened?

➤ When has this happened?

➤ How has this happened?

➤ What do you think will happen next?

➤ What clues support your view?

19 Skimming and scanning

> *Never confuse a single defeat with a final defeat.*
>
> Francis Scott Fitzgerald (1896–1940), American novelist

Skimming and scanning are essential skills to acquire especially when studying for exams, answering questions or writing essays. When surrounded by what seems like every book ever published, one needs to know how to skim and scan.

Skimming is used to locate the main ideas of a piece of writing. When you skim read something you tend to read it three or four times faster than you would if you were reading. So how do you do it? Well, you can read the opening and closing paragraphs by looking at the subheadings as you work your way down the text or you can read the opening sentence of each paragraph. Often it helps to use a highlighter to highlight the key facts as you read. Skimming is a good technique, especially when looking to locate places, dates and names.

Scanning is often what you do when you're looking up a word in a dictionary—you use it when you search for key ideas or words. When scanning a text you usually move your eyes quickly down the page looking for key words or phrases to answer questions.

- Introduce task and the skill of skimming and scanning. Discuss with the class how to skim and scan effectively.
- Put students into teams of two or three.
- Each team to be given a list of questions—the answers can be located from the information stuck on the classroom walls (this could be on a topic that is being studied at the moment).
- The aim is for students to locate and select the appropriate information required in the time given.
- The teacher and two other student experts (in skimming and scanning) are to observe students and how they approach this task.
- To help students with this task, there is a table containing resources such as highlighters, Post-its, etc.
- When a group has completed the questions, the activity stops and the whole class gives feedback.
- The student experts then offer feedback about strategies used and ways forward for students to improve their skimming and scanning techniques.

Cross-curricular:

- Suitable for any subject.
- Needed in all subjects!
- Although the focus of this task is skimming and scanning, you are also revising your chosen topic.

Why use this strategy?

- Skimming and scanning is essential in all subjects—so practice, practice, practice!
- For every subject students will need to be able to read and locate information—acquiring this skill will make learning easier.
- It's fun!
- It's kinaesthetic!
- It's inclusive as everyone has to contribute.
- It requires students to be critical of other students' work in a constructive manner.
- It highlights the importance of working together as a team to locate the clues—joint responsibility.
- It encourages students to work together as they have a deadline to meet!

Creativity and critical thinking – learning to learn skills:

- Learning with and from others
- Thinking

20 Book corner

> *The reading of all good books is like conversation with the finest men of the past centuries.*
>
> René Descartes (1596–1650), French philosopher

It is important that students recognise that reading is something to be done in all subjects and is not just an English subject requirement. Therefore if all subjects could have a book box (containing relevant magazines and newspapers as well as fact and fiction books) in the corner of their classroom for students to read, this would make reading a more familiar pastime.

- Every two weeks, allow students to choose a book which interests them from the book box—it may be fact or fiction.
- Students to spend the first five minutes of every lesson reading their subject-specific book whilst the rest of the class are arriving or unpacking.
- Once a fortnight students present to the class about the books they have been reading:
  – What they are about.
  – What they have learnt.
  – Would they recommend it to other students and why.
- Whilst a student is presenting their book, the rest of the class write down questions about the book to ask when the presentation is over.

Cross-curricular:

- At the start of each topic the teacher recommends books to students which they would benefit from reading.
- Allow a couple of students to be known as the book corner experts. They are to ensure that all students are up to speed with the specific literacy skills being developed.
- Get students to display book reviews of their favourite books around the room.

Why use this strategy?

- It encourages reading!
- It widens students' knowledge about book types.
- It's a good way of developing students' knowledge of the subject beyond the curriculum.
- It's a good way of revising cross-curricular literacy skills.

Creativity and critical thinking - learning to learn skills:

- Learning with and from others
- Investigating resources

21 Window shopping!

> *Words are the voice of the heart.*
>
> Confucius (551–479 BC), Chinese philosopher

A good way to develop your reading strategy is to think about reading as though you are going shopping. OK, so here we go …

- Shop window (observe what is around).
- Ask questions about products (go in, root around—ask yourself 'Is this the answer to my clothes dreams?')
- Read the price tag!
- Gulp!!!! (in response to those numbers).
- Let's work this out (review all the information gathered—is this what you were looking for?).

So let's put this into practice. Students can do this individually but it's probably more fun in pairs.

- Give students a text.
- The aim of the task is for students to read the text and then locate the information within by using the window shopping strategy above.
- So: shop window is skimming and scanning; ask questions is 'how does this relate to the question?'; price tag is study the text in greater detail; gulp is gulp!; and review is let's bring it all together to answer the question being asked.

Cross-curricular:

- Suitable for any subject.
- This skill can be used at any point during a topic to test students' understanding.
- Videoing the process and showing the video back to the students would be a good way to get them to reflect upon their strengths and areas to be developed.

Why use this strategy?

- It's another strategy which helps students develop their reading skills.
- It's fun!
- It relates the issue of locating and selecting resources to the well-known pains of shopping! Hard work!
- Working in groups helps to develop students' learning to learn skills, provided they look at the learning process they went through.
- Students are continually reflecting throughout this process.
- It's metacognitive.

Creativity and critical thinking – learning to learn skills:

- Learning with and from others
- Thinking

22 Crosswords and Sudoku

> *Reading is to the mind, what exercise is to the body.*
>
> Joseph Addison (1672–1719), English poet and essayist

There are many fun techniques that we as teachers can use to address students' understanding of reading. Crosswords and Sudoku are two of them. Both are word or number puzzles which take the shape of a square which is made up of small black and white squares. The aim is for all the small squares to be filled with words or numbers by solving a series of clues.

- Students to be given a list of questions in crossword or Sudoku form. In order to answer the questions, students will need to do some research using computers and reference books.
- Students to work in groups of three or four to research a topic given by the teacher in a given time limit. The research will enable students to answer the questions given at the start of the lesson. Each student within the group is to research a specific area so that they can become an expert in that arena.
- After the time limit, the group come together and share their knowledge.
- One person from each group is to move to another group and share their expert knowledge and gather the expert knowledge from the new group. All students to take notes of their classmates' expertise.
- All students to return to their original groups and share new knowledge.
- All groups to complete crosswords or Sudoku-based questions upon facts learnt. As soon as one group has answered the crossword or Sudoku the activity stops.

Cross-curricular:

- Any subject can use these strategies, provided the teacher can locate appropriate resources.
- In some subjects, it might be more suitable if groups are smaller, i.e. pairs.
- The teacher could be a resource and a student could be in control of managing the activity—building on their learning to learn skills.
- In Maths and Physics, you might want to change the title to Sudoku.

Why use these strategies?

- The overriding purpose of this technique is to improve students' reading—because it has a fun factor to it, this should help to motivate students and improve learning.
- Deep learning occurs when the brain can make sense of things for itself. As the students are creating a personal construct, in addition to the discussion taking place, this will help to cement the learning in their minds.
- Exam results will improve.
- Sudoku might be a good option for Maths lessons!
- This activity has a kinaesthetic element to it, which is vital for some students as it keeps them focused.

- It reminds us that learning can be more effective when students are locating and selecting relevant information, rather than it being given to them.
- It allows students to develop their independent and interdependent skills to work well within a group as well as by themselves.

Creativity and critical thinking – learning to learn skills:

- Learning with and from others
- Investigating resources

23 Roll the dice!

> *A word of encouragement during a failure is worth more than an hour of praise after success.*
>
> **Anonymous**

This is a great strategy when introducing a new topic. It reminds us how important it is to examine the whole picture and look at things from every angle.

- Write the name of the new topic on the board and call upon a student to roll a dice—this student should be the topic expert.
- Students are put into teams of four so they can confer about answers.
- All teams will be asked questions which are based on a prior text reading.
- The number the dice falls on will determine which question will be asked to the class about the chosen topic:

Dice:	Meaning:
1.	Explain topic.
2.	Reasons for and reasons against topic.
3.	What does it remind you of?
4.	What is it made up of—ingredients?
5.	Has it changed over time?
6.	Where do you see its future?

- The scoring for each question will be as follows: two points for each correct question and one point if the question is handed over to another team to answer and they answer it correctly.
- When the game is over, discussion is led by the dice expert about the strengths of group-work used during this strategy and the knowledge which needs to be revised.

Cross-curricular:

- Suitable for all subjects and for analysing new topics.
- Science—good when starting experiments.
- PE—good for introducing new sports topics.
- Humanities—good for introducing new topics and so on.
- Good for learning to learn as this strategy promotes thinking and groupwork.

Why use this strategy?

- The overriding purpose of this strategy is to provide another avenue for students to use to maximise their reading.
- Encourages students to think.
- Helps students to organise their thoughts.
- It's fun.
- It promotes learning to learn and students working in groups.

Creativity and critical thinking – learning to learn skills:

- Learning with and from others
- Thinking

24 Circles cascade!

> *You can teach a student a lesson for a day; but if you can teach him to learn by creating curiosity, he will continue the learning process as long as he lives.*
>
> **Anonymous**

This strategy allows students to be aware of the key ideas and details which arise when reading.

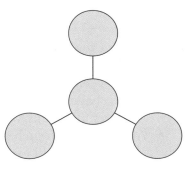

- Having read a text, put students into pairs. Students to draw the diagram opposite—if they wish to extend the diagram with further circles they may do so.
- In the top circle students write the topic being studied. In each circle which follows underneath they write the key points from the text they have just absorbed—from the most important to the least important.
- It is worthwhile getting students to use poster paper to carry out this activity, so they don't feel their ideas are limited by the size of the paper.
- Display work and get students to explain the key points they chose.

Cross-curricular:

- Suitable for any subject where students need to understand key ideas.
- This is a quick way of assessing students' understanding.
- If students are computer literate they can complete this task on a computer.
- Display work—this boosts self-esteem and you can refer to it when discussing the topic.

Why use this strategy?

- This is another strategy for developing students' reading—allowing them a visual image of the content of the text read.
- Good for revision.
- Good for assessing students' understanding of prior learning.
- Deep learning occurs because the brain is making sense of the information.
- This strategy requires the brain to be active and engaged.
- This strategy is good for developing learning to learn as thinking and groupwork skills are being developed.

Creativity and critical thinking – learning to learn skills:

- Learning with and from others
- Thinking

25 What's your problem?

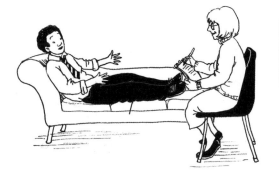

> *Today a reader, tomorrow a leader.*
> Margaret Fuller (1810–50), American journalist

- Students to be given a challenge (suitable for numerical challenges) to solve in small groups.
- Teacher to reinforce the rule:
  - Find the challenge.
  - What questions help you answer the challenge?
  - How can we use this information to solve the initial challenge?
- Often challenges can be solved a lot quicker if we break them down into smaller parts then step back and look at the bigger picture—have a go!
- After the challenge has been solved, the first team to finish the task share the solution with the class and explain the skills they used to solve the problem.

Cross-curricular:

- Good for Science, Maths, Design and Technology.
- Good for subjects in which students regularly need to solve a challenge.
- Promotes learning to learn through thinking skills.
- Promotes learning to learn through the skills needed to learn with and from others.
- Perfect for ensuring that students understand what has been learnt.

Why use this strategy?

- Another good strategy for students to use to tackle reading challenges.
- Good exam preparation.
- Good for creating deep learning because the brain is making sense of the information.
- This strategy requires the brain to be active and engaged.

Creativity and critical thinking – learning to learn skills:

- Planning
- Thinking

26 Finding the clues

This is a good strategy to use to help students who struggle to access text.

- In pairs, pupils to be given a text and a series of questions to answer.
- If students feel they cannot answer the questions set, they are allowed to use the clues envelope—provided the teacher thinks this is necessary.
- Inside the clues envelope are cut out slips. On the slips are incomplete sentences with key words missing, which will answer the questions, provided the missing words are added. Students will need to choose which answer goes with which question and will need to locate the missing words from the original text.
- Some students will need additional help and they will be permitted to look at the clue 2 envelope which contains the missing words. As in the previous stage of the game, they will need to locate which words go with which sentence.
- And so the game continues.
- As soon as a group finishes the game, the game is over.
- Teacher to go over all the answers with the whole class and discuss the strategies students used to answer the questions.

Cross-curricular:

- At the start of each topic allow a couple of students to be known as the experts of this literacy area. They are to ensure that all students are up to speed with any specific literacy skills being developed during the lesson.
- Quick revision of literacy elements in the topics being studied.
- It might be worthwhile getting students to write down strategies to use to work through this type of literacy skill.

Why use this strategy?

- Excellent for learning to learn as students develop groupwork skills—provided you discuss the key facts.
- It's inclusive—all students must get involved.
- It's a good way of revising literacy skills across the curriculum.

Creativity and critical thinking - learning to learn skills:

- Learning with and from others
- Thinking

27 Guided writing – What do I need?

> *The pen is the tongue of the mind.*
>
> **Miguel de Cervantes (1547–1616), Spanish writer**

This activity is to get students actively involved in thinking about what and how they write. It allows students to be supported in the writing process at different stages.

- Class discussion about techniques needed for guided writing (use the 'Guided writing checklist' proforma below).
- Give students a writing task on the topic being studied at present.
- Before students start writing, the teacher pulls from a hat the 'before you start writing questions' (see 'Guided writing checklist' proforma). Class discussion about what points you must consider before you start writing. Students to complete the first part of the 'Student self-help sheet for guided writing' proforma (see below).
- Students to begin writing task. Students only given half the total writing time and then stopped by the teacher. Students asked to proofread their work. Then the teacher pulls out from a hat the 'whilst you are writing questions' (see 'Guided writing checklist' proforma). Class discussion about these questions. Students reminded that it is important that they consider these points before they continue writing. Students to complete the second part of the 'Student self-help sheet for guided writing' proforma.
- Students given the remainder of the time to complete the task and then teacher pulls out from a hat the 'are you sure you've finished writing questions' (see 'Guided writing checklist' proforma). Class discussion about these questions. Students reminded that it is important that they consider these points before they decide their work is finished. Students to complete the final part of the 'Student self-help sheet for guided writing' proforma.
- Students to self-check work—checking it against the 'Student self-help sheet for guided writing' proforma.
- Another student to proofread work—checking it against the 'Guided writing checklist' proforma.

Cross-curricular:

- Suitable for any subject that requires writing!
- Good for promoting thinking and then transferring thinking skills across subjects!
- Although the focus of this task is guided writing, you are also revising your chosen topic.

Why use this strategy?

- It gets students thinking more actively about what is being asked of them when writing.
- Good way to revise topics.
- Moulds students into constructive critics of their work—resulting in them setting targets to improve.
- It's inclusive.
- It encourages students to write at the depth that is required.

Creativity and critical thinking – learning to learn skills:

- Learning with and from others
- Planning
- Thinking

■ Guided writing checklist

Before you start writing questions:
- What is the point of what I am doing—purpose?
- What have I been asked to do?
- Who am I writing this for—audience?
- Will this piece of writing have an impact upon its readers?
- What do I call this writing type?
- What do I need to include in this piece of writing to make it successful?
- How will I organise my ideas?
- What am I going to include in my introduction, middle and conclusion?

Whilst you are writing questions:
- Does what I've written make sense?
- Have I used capital letters and full stops correctly?
- Have I arranged my sentences into paragraphs?
- How do I want the reader to feel at this point?
- Do I need to add examples?
- Am I concise in my writing or do I waffle?
- Do I vary my sentence lengths?
- Do I use long words?
- Do I use connectives?
- Are my points linked?
- Do I use evidence such as statistics to strengthen my point?
- Do I use alliteration and other poetic devices?
- Do I state facts and opinions?
- Do I use repetition?
- Do I use emotive language and the 'rule of three'?
- Do I use a range of punctuation?

Are you sure you've finished writing questions:
- Have I answered the question?
- Does the opening encourage the reader to read on?
- Does the conclusion make the reader want to read further?
- Have I proofread my work for punctuation, sentence length, missing words and spelling?
- Do my paragraphs link?

■ Student self-help sheet for guided writing

Name:

Subject:

Before you start writing questions:

Points	My response
What is the point of what you are doing— purpose?	
What have you been asked to do?	
Who are you writing this for—audience?	
Will this piece of writing have an impact upon its readers?	
What do we call this writing type?	
What do we need to include in this piece of writing to make it successful?	
How will you organise your ideas?	
What are you going to include in your introduction, middle and conclusion?	

Whilst you are writing questions:

Points	My response
Does what you've written make sense?	
Have I used capital letters and full stops correctly?	
Have I arranged my sentences into paragraphs?	
How do I want the reader to feel at this point?	
Do I need to add examples?	
Am I concise in my writing or do I waffle?	

Points	My response
Do I vary my sentence lengths?	
Do I use long words?	
Do I use connectives?	
Are my points linked?	
Do I use evidence such as statistics to strengthen my point?	
Do I use alliteration and other poetic devices?	
Do I state facts and opinions?	
Do I use repetition?	
Do I use emotive language and the 'rule of three'?	
Do I use a range of punctuation?	

Are you sure you've finished writing questions:

Points	My response
Have I answered the question?	
Does the opening encourage the reader to read on?	
Does the conclusion make the reader want to read further?	
Have I proofread my work for punctuation, sentence length, missing words and spelling?	
Do my paragraphs link?	

28 Writing frame – Writing a balanced argument

Between my finger and my thumb the squat pen rests. I'll dig with it.

Seamus Heaney (1939–), Irish poet

Students need to be able to write a balanced argument. In life, it is important that we can express our opinions in a calm and balanced manner. In order to do that, it is vital they show an understanding of how to structure writing, making effective use of connected paragraphs.

- Teacher to stick on the classroom walls different argument titles suited to the topic being studied at present.
- In groups of three, students to walk around the room and pick an argument title topic.
- Class discussion about what makes a balanced argument.
- Each group of students to plan a balanced argument (see 'Writing frame' proforma below) focusing on the title they selected. Students to fill out the proforma.
- After filling out the proforma, each group must prepare a role play, which will consist of the following characters: judge, prosecutor and defender. The characters act out their chosen argument as though they are in a court room.
- The prosecutor and defender present their viewpoints but it is the judge's duty to hear both viewpoints fairly.
- When the teacher shouts 'Order! Order!' the groups perform their role plays in front of the class. After the performances, discussion is held about the language and structure of a balanced argument. Students in each group make any necessary changes to their plan based upon their performance and the class discussion.
- In their groups, students write a balanced argument on the initial chosen topic.

Cross-curricular:

- This is a great way to get students to see both sides of a debate for all subjects.
- This can be used for any subject.
- The stimulus will be material from your subject area, so it is an effective revision tool.
- At the start of the lesson ask students how balanced arguments might be used in your subject area.

Why use this strategy?

- It's a good strategy to get students to understand the key areas needed for a balanced argument.
- As this strategy promotes groupwork it lends itself to learning to learn skills.
- As drama is involved in this activity, it suits students who are visual and kinaesthetic learners.
- It allows students to develop their social skills.
- Students often learn better from each other.

Creativity and critical thinking – learning to learn skills:

- Learning with and from others
- Planning
- Thinking

■ Writing frame for a balanced argument

Explain what the title is—what is the issue?
Introduce the issue and its importance:
Explain people's reasons for and against the issue in sequence. Remember to use connectives and emotive language and keep your argument balanced. Helpful phrases which link one point to the next might include: *in addition ... also ... furthermore ... moreover ... on the other hand ...*
Sum up the main points:
Conclusion:

29 Writing to argue

> *Language is power ... Language can be used as a means of changing reality.*
>
> Adrienne Rich (1929–) American poet

Writing to argue shows evidence of a well-reasoned viewpoint as well as trying to counter opposing viewpoints.

- Students to be given a heading, for example, '*Top Gear* is the best programme that ever existed!'
- In groups, students to create a list of features of argumentative writing (see 'Writing frame for argumentative writing' proforma below). Whole class to discuss the list created.
- Students, in pairs, to be given a topic related to what they are studying at the moment and to create a plan for their writing which argues either for or against that topic. Students to write their plan on the proforma.
- Pairs given five minutes to write the beginning of their argumentative piece of writing, then an additional one minute to proofread and then pass on their work to another group.
- Every group should read someone else's work.
- Students given a further five minutes to add comments to the written work—what to add to ensure it is an effective argumentative piece of writing, as well as adding two positive comments.
- All work should be displayed and strengths and areas to develop discussed.

Cross-curricular:

- Understanding argumentative texts is an important life skill required for reading and writing, irrespective of the subject.
- This is a suitable strategy for revising a topic.
- This is a suitable strategy for checking the understanding of a new topic.

Why use this strategy?

- A good strategy for students to develop their argumentative writing style.
- It helps students sequence ideas in a logical way.
- It encourages students to use various connectives.
- It encourages students to use and think about cause and effect.
- It encourages students to be critical thinkers.
- It develops students' learning to learn skills as they work in groups, although it is important that they reflect upon their strengths and areas to develop.

Creativity and critical thinking – learning to learn skills:

- Learning with and from others
- Planning
- Thinking

■ Writing frame for argumentative writing

Title:
Explain what you are arguing for:
Explain why this is important—give evidence:
Give examples:
Explain the counter-arguments:
Conclusion:

- Structure is very important—draw a diagram beforehand if that helps. Remember to proofread and use time-based connectives. Also, begin a new paragraph every time you start to show a change in time, event or place. Use language to impress and convince the reader of your viewpoint.

30 Writing frame - Writing instructions

> *Education is the most powerful weapon which you can use to change the world.*
>
> Nelson Mandela (1918–), Nobel Peace Prize winner and former President of South Africa

Students need to know how to write instructions. It is important that they use the writing conventions expected of them. They need to ensure that the writing is aimed at the correct audience, that tone and vocabulary are suited to the purpose and that the instructions are organised in a logical sequence. Examples of instructions might be: recipes (Home Economics), experiments (Science), directions (Geography/MFL) and so on.

- Stick five sheets of paper on the wall numbered 1, 2, 3, 4 and 5. Also stick on the wall an example of a writing frame for writing instructions (see proforma below).
- Stick a set of instructions onto sheets 2, 3 and 4—this must be the same set of instructions on all three sheets of paper.
- Divide students into groups numbered 1 to 5.
- Ask Group 1 to go to sheet 1 and brainstorm all the conventions for writing instructions. Group 2 to go to sheet 2, which has a set of instructions on it, and using Post-its and highlighters explain the conventions used. Group 3 is to highlight the strengths of the same set of instructions on sheet 3. Group 4 is to highlight the weaknesses of the same set of instructions on sheet 4. Group 5 uses sheet 5 to design a writing frame for instructions.
- Each group has five minutes at their numbered sheet to complete their task. When the time limit is up, they move to the next sheet until they have visited and commented on every sheet.
- A spokesperson from each group talks to the class about each of the five numbered sheets.
- Class discussion about the 'perfect set of instructions' is held—emphasis on the literacy element is vital.
- Students to write their own set of instructions on a topic relevant to what they are studying at present.

Cross-curricular:

- This can be used for any subject.
- The instructions you use as a stimulus will be instructions from your subject area.
- At the start of the lesson ask students how instructions might be used in your subject area.

Why use this strategy?

- Reinforces rules learnt about writing instructions.
- Promotes groupwork and therefore develops students' learning to learn skills.
- Suits students who are visual and kinaesthetic learners.
- One of the benefits of this type of activity is that it creates a student-centred starting point.
- Students develop social skills.
- Students often learn better from each other.

Creativity and critical thinking – learning to learn skills:

- Learning with and from others
- Planning
- Thinking

■ Writing frame for writing instructions

Explain what the instructions are for (the purpose):
Explain what the ingredients are:
Explain what you will need to do to make the item. Do this in the order that you will need to do it (you might find it helpful to use bullet points or numbers) and also list the materials you will need.
Explain what the end product will be:
Explain any technical terms:
Warn the reader about any potential problems that could arise:
Suggest to the reader what they could go on to make after this:

Remember to use verbs, especially to start your sentences, and connectives such as firstly
... *or* next ...

31 Persuasive writing

Language makes so many things possible.

Margaret Meek (1925–), Emeritus Professor, University of London Institute of Education

One of the key points of persuasive writing is the ability to use positive images and statements which will make the reader feel drawn to the viewpoint being presented.

- Put students into groups of four and give out the 'Persuasive writing frame' proforma (see below).
- Give students a text about the topic being studied at the moment.
- Students to read the text, annotate it and consider the following points:
  - What is the text about?
  - What is the purpose of the text?
  - Who is the target audience?
- As a group discuss the following:
  - punctuation
  - layout
  - use of columns
  - headings/subheadings
  - statistics
  - alliteration
  - quotes
  - repetition
  - emotive language
  - 'rule of three'.
- Groups to annotate the text, making points about the impact of the above techniques.
- All groups to pass their annotated text to the group to the right. Groups to note the points made by the previous group and to add further annotations and comments about points they agree and disagree with. Students should complete the 'Students' check grid for persuasive writing' proforma (see below) whilst they are doing this part of the activity.
- Students' work is passed around and annotated by the other student groups until every group has seen and commented on everybody's work.
- Persuasive writing literacy expert to lead discussion about persuasive writing techniques.

Cross-curricular:

- Some subjects are more suited to persuasive writing than others. However, the skills required are important life skills that students will need.
- This strategy is good for revising any topic.
- This is a good strategy for developing analytical thinking.

Why use this strategy?

- Students need to know the skills required for persuasive writing and this reinforces the key skills needed.
- The more examples students are subjected to, the more chance they will use the skills required.
- This strategy encourages students to be constructively critical of their work.
- It encourages students to think about their choices of persuasive language.

Creativity and critical thinking – learning to learn skills:

- Learning with and from others
- Planning
- Thinking
- Investigating resources

■ Persuasive writing frame

Remember to reflect upon what you have written—stop and reflect throughout the writing process.

Title:
Opening statement about the persuasive topic (continue this with a general opening and information about the topic):
Ask a question to draw the reader in:
State three positives about your topic (facts, opinions, benefits):
State opposing views and why they are misguided:
Ask a question and tell the reader how to get involved:
Conclusion. Make it powerful and draw the reader back to your main points:

■ Students' check grid for persuasive writing

Points to consider	Tick if done	Comments
Is it clear what the text is about?		
Is the purpose of the text clear?		
Is it clear who the audience are?		
Have you used a powerful introduction?		
Have you used appropriate and varied punctuation?		
Have you used an appropriate layout (have you considered the writing frame)?		
Have you used statistics?		
Have you used questions to draw the reader in?		
Have you stated positives about your topic and explained them?		
Have you mentioned the negatives and presented them in a new light so they do not seem as bad?		
Have you used alliteration?		
Have you used quotes?		
Have you used emotive writing?		
Have you used the 'rule of three'?		
Have you used a powerful conclusion?		

32 Writing to explain

Darren doesn't have his homework because he was sick. Signed, My Mum

> *When you sell a man a book you don't sell him just 12 ounces of paper and ink and glue—you sell him a whole new life.*
>
> Christopher Morley (1890–1957), American journalist

Students will always need to be able to explain. It is important when writing to explain that the information is useful and accessible as well as balanced and truthful. This strategy reinforces the skills already learnt for them to succeed in writing to explain.

- Students to be given a heading, for example, 'How a Formula 1 car works'. Class discussion about how they would explain the answer to that question—what language techniques would they need to include in their writing?
- In groups, students to create a list of features for explanation writing (see 'Writing frame for explanation writing' proforma below). Class discussion about the features needed for explanation writing.
- Students, in pairs, to be given a topic related to what they are studying at the moment and asked to create a piece of writing which explains that topic.
- Students given five minutes to write about the topic and a further one minute to proof-read. Then they must pass the work on to another pair, anti-clockwise.
- Every group should read someone else's work.
- Students given five minutes to add comments about what to add to ensure it is an effective piece of explanation writing, as well as adding two positive comments.
- All work should be displayed and strengths and areas to develop discussed.

Cross-curricular:

- Understanding explanation texts is an important life skill required for reading and writing, irrespective of the subject.
- This is a suitable strategy for revising a topic.
- This is a suitable strategy for checking the understanding of a new topic.

Why use this strategy?

- Good strategy for students to develop their ability to write to explain.
- Helps students sequence ideas in a logical way.
- Encourages students to use various connectives.
- Encourages students to use and think about cause and effect.
- Encourages students to be critical thinkers.
- Develops students' learning to learn skills as students work in groups, although it is important that they reflect upon their strengths and areas to develop.

Creativity and critical thinking – learning to learn skills:

- Learning with and from others
- Planning
- Thinking

■ Writing frame for explanation writing

Title:
Describe what you are explaining (usually the words how/why are necessary):
Explain what it is (use subheadings if necessary):
What happens (remember it is important to explain events in time order or cause and effect)?
Why does it happen?
How does it happen?
Explain the result (use time-based connectives, e.g. Next ...):
Conclusion:

Remember to use time-based connectives and technical vocabulary. Also, begin a new paragraph every time you show a change in time, event or place.

33 Writing to recount

Being able to recount is an important skill for many subjects. What follows is a strategy which will help to reinforce the skills needed to write to recount successfully.

- Give students a factual or fictional event relevant to the subject being studied and ask them to recount it orally to their neighbour.
- Ask students to write down what they know about recount writing.
- Students to compare notes with their neighbours.
- A student volunteer shares their ideas with the rest of the class and gains the expert of recount writing title. Class allowed to comment on the ideas given—both positive and ways to develop. (If the expert is stuck and another student is willing to take over the title can be passed over.)
- Teacher to give students a topic which involves students being able to draw upon their prior knowledge to write a recount piece of writing.
- In pairs, students plan and fill out the 'Recount writing frame' proforma (see below) about the topic the teacher has given them.
- Once the proforma is filled out, ideas can be shared with the class.
- The class expert and teacher to begin modelling the writing of the topic.

Cross-curricular:

- This is a suitable strategy for revising a topic.
- This is a suitable strategy for checking the understanding of a new topic.
- It encourages students to use and think about cause and effect.

Why use this strategy?

- Being able to recount correctly is an important life skill required for reading and writing, irrespective of the subject.
- It encourages students to use various connectives.
- It helps students to sequence ideas in a logical way.
- It encourages students to be critical thinkers.
- It develops students' learning to learn skills as students work in groups, although it is important that they reflect upon their strengths and areas to develop.

Creativity and critical thinking – learning to learn skills:

- Learning with and from others
- Planning
- Thinking

■ Recount writing frame

Title:
What happened? Remember to describe events in sequential order, use verbs in the past tense and write in either the first or third person.
Where does it happen? Use paragraphs to show movement between point/time/place and event. Remember to use time-based connectives.
Who does it involve?
What do they say?
How do they feel?
Conclusion. An important paragraph which should highlight the importance of these incidents.

34 Writing to advise

Dear Miserable of 8B...

> *The six golden rules of writing: read, read, read, and write, write, write.*
>
> **Ernest Gaines (1933–), African-American fiction writer**

Students will always need to write to advise. What follows is a strategy to help students improve their understanding of this skill.

- Students to be given a heading, for example, 'It's important to be fit and healthy; therefore you should play sports at least three times per week'. Class discussion about how to answer this question.
- In groups, students to create a list of features for writing to advise (see 'Writing frame for advice writing' below).
- Students, in pairs, to be given a topic related to what they are studying at the moment and asked to create a piece of writing which explains how it works.
- Students given five minutes to write on this topic and a further one minute to proofread their work. Then they must pass the work on to another group.
- Every group should read someone else's work.
- Students given a further five minutes to add comments about what to add to ensure it is an effective piece of writing to advise. In addition, each pair must write two positive comments about the work.
- All work should be displayed and strengths and areas to develop discussed.

Cross-curricular:

- Understanding advisory texts is an important life skill required for reading and writing, irrespective of the subject.
- This is a suitable strategy for revising a topic.
- This is a suitable strategy for checking the understanding of a new topic.

Why use this strategy?

- Good strategy for students to develop their ability to write to advise.
- It helps students sequence ideas in a logical way.
- It encourages students to use various connectives.
- It encourages students to use and think about cause and effect.
- It encourages students to be critical thinkers.
- It develops students' learning to learn skills as students work in groups, although it is important that they reflect upon their strengths and areas to develop.

Creativity and critical thinking – learning to learn skills:

- Learning with and from others
- Planning
- Thinking

■ **Writing frame for advice writing**

Title:
Explain what you are advising:
Explain why you are advising this: Do this first. Then you might want to consider ...
Be encouraging—give evidence that this is this best for them. Be clear, e.g. Don't worry, Be positive, Alternatively...
Give a choice of alternatives. Be polite!
Explain the outcome if they do as you have advised.
Conclusion. End by encouraging your reader to carry out the advice you have suggested.

Remember to proofread and use time-based connectives. Also, begin a new paragraph every time you start to show a change in time, event or place.

35 Instant response

No skill is more crucial to the future of a child, or to a democratic and prosperous society, than literacy.

Michael Parks, 'A Long Road Back From Reading Crisis', *Los Angeles Times*, 13 September 1998

In some subjects, students are expected to work at a higher level whilst being introduced to another skill. This strategy looks at ways to develop their ability to respond instantly to questions about their learning.

- Provide students with A4 paper and ask them to write their answers to the following questions (one about subject content and one about a literacy skill being studied at the moment):
  - What have you learnt?
  - What have been the challenges?
  - Have you understood what you are learning?
  The only criteria for students whilst answering the questions is for them to write in complete sentences.
- Students have two minutes to answer each question.
- This strategy works best if you give students one question, get them to write an answer and then get them to give feedback.
- Students to answer questions on coloured card. Colours denote their level of understanding of learning:
  - Sunny yellow – good
  - Rainy grey – uncertain
  - Black thunder – no learning taking place.
- After each question discuss the points raised.

Cross-curricular:

- This strategy can be used for measuring students' learning in any subject.
- This strategy can be used at any point during the lesson—and can be used several times during the lesson to ensure students are learning.
- It's a good strategy to promote thinking and therefore learning to learn.

Why use this strategy?

- It encourages students to think about their learning.
- It promotes student voice.
- It promotes learning to learn.
- It allows the teacher a quick overview of students' learning.

Creativity and critical thinking – learning to learn skills:

- Learning with and from others
- Planning
- Thinking

36 Annotating

> *Language is the dress of thought.*
> Samuel Johnson (1709–84), English author

Annotating is an important tool to help us identify the key points in a text. We can annotate by underlining or highlighting key words and phrases, making notes in the margin, commenting on interesting features and patterns (and asking ourselves why), such as repetition, comparisons and contrasts.

- Introduce the task and begin with a class discussion about the skills required when annotating.
- In pairs, students to be given a piece of text which they are expected to annotate.
- It's best if the text is stuck onto a bigger sheet of paper so they can annotate on the bigger sheet using arrows etc.
- Once the time limit is up, they pass their annotated work on to another group.
- Students must add to what other groups have written but also cross out annotations if they disagree with them—but writing comments explaining their actions.
- When the time is up, the work is passed on to another group and the game continues until the work is back with the original authors.
- Class discussion about comments written.

Cross-curricular:

- Good strategy for checking understanding of a topic.
- Possible to use this strategy when introducing a new topic.
- At the start of each topic allow a couple of students to be known as the experts of that literacy area—they are to ensure that all students are up to speed with the specific literacy skills being developed.
- Remember to display the skills needed for annotation on your walls.

Why use this strategy?

- Annotation is an important reading strategy for most subjects and this will help students improve this skill.
- Deep learning occurs when the mind is thinking—this strategy should strengthen students' learning.
- It encourages teamwork and develops groupwork skills—it is therefore excellent for learning to learn.
- It's a good way of revising cross-curricular literacy skills.
- It's a good way of learning or revising a new topic.

Creativity and critical thinking - learning to learn skills:

- Learning with and from others
- Thinking

37 Writing frame for story writing

> *Tell me and I'll forget; show me and I may remember; involve me and I'll understand.*
>
> **Chinese proverb**

It is important that students can write stories. What follows is a strategy that can be used to improve students' understanding of story writing.

- Class discussion about the skills required for story writing (see 'Planning creative writing frame' proforma below).
- Put students in teams of four.
- Teacher to shuffle a deck of cards. On each deck are characters for students to include in their story. Characters can relate to the topic being studied at the moment.
- Once students have been given cards, group to brainstorm ideas for writing frame.
- In each team, students to have the following roles:

Job title:	Description:
Writer	Writes the story
Plot maker	Devises the twists and turns in the story
Language maker	Incorporates language which makes the story believable
Critical thinker	Ensures all targets have been met

- After students have finished writing, in the time limit given, they must proofread and check work against the proforma.
- All students in group must have carried out their roles actively.
- Groups to swap work with other groups and let them mark it against the proforma.

Cross-curricular:

- It is possible to change characters on cards to setting or brief outline of plot.
- Get students to create characters for cards—get them involved.
- Good for subjects which require story writing include Humanities, English and Drama.
- It is possible to use this strategy in subjects such as Science and Technology, though you will have to be creative.

Why use this strategy?

- Good for getting students to recognise the skills needed for creative writing.
- Good for getting students to be critical of their work.
- It encourages the development of the learning to learn skills as students are thinking and working in groups—just remember to get them talking about their learning with regards to these skills.

Creativity and critical thinking – learning to learn skills:

- Learning with and from others
- Planning
- Thinking

■ Planning creative writing frame

Title:
Who are the characters? Why will we want to read about them?
Where does the action happen?
Plot?
Twist?
Ending?

38 Speaking through finger puppets

> *Speech is power: speech is to persuade, to convert, to compel.*
>
> Ralph Waldo Emerson (1803–82), American writer

Good speaking is a combination of good ideas, structure and confidence. Speaking happens in all lessons and in all walks of life, so it is essential that students get it right.

- Put students into groups of four.
- Give all students either a piece of cloth or a piece of paper and get them to make a finger puppet, but as they make it, each student must explain to the group how they are creating it.
- One pupil in the group records who is the most successful at explaining and why. Class discussion about this.
- Each pupil to decide who their finger puppet is—it must be a famous person from that subject area (alive or dead) or a teacher. Each pupil to explain their puppet person's history or, in the case of a teacher, to teach the group a topic being studied at present (presentations to last no longer than three minutes).
- One student from each group to re-present their finger puppet presentation but this time to the whole class—these students become the experts.
- The class is allowed to ask questions about the presentation to the student presenting (every student should aim to ask at least one question).
- Another finger puppet expert is brought up to the front to re-perform and so the process continues.

Cross-curricular:

- Give students 15 seconds to think of an answer to a question before they are allowed to put their hand up—for some students it might be worthwhile getting them to share their answer with their neighbour before they share it with the whole class.
- If students are shy of contributing try to get them to speak three times in each lesson and record a tick in the margin of their book each time they contribute—you can raise the number of ticks as their confidence grows.
- Videoing students when they are talking is a good way for the whole class to evaluate their strengths and areas to develop—although you might need to use some brave students for this one!
- Reinforce the idea that students must structure their speaking like an essay—so it has a beginning (introduce the topic), middle (use evidence and explain) and ending (sum up). In a sense, it is just like story writing.
- Have a 'Talking Week' in school (see Strategy 44)—no writing and all learning must be through speech. A great activity for all involved!

Why use this strategy?

- It hooks students in and can be quite moving to watch.
- Students who are unsure about some areas of a subject will learn more through this fun medium—it gives access to information to all learning abilities.
- As this is a dynamic and relatively unusual strategy, students tend to remember it.

Creativity and critical thinking - learning to learn skills:

- Planning
- Thinking

39 Circle - Who am I?

Speaking and listening are essential literacy and life skills. This strategy promotes speaking in a safe environment.

- Clear the desks to the side of the classroom and arrange the chairs into a circle.
- Students to sit in a circle.
- Invite students to begin by clapping to a slow beat. The aim of the game is for everyone in the circle to talk when it is their turn in between the claps which will need to be kept to a rhythm.
- Some less able students may need to use the literacy prompts (see below).
- Invite a student to begin. That student states their name and favourite literacy element (e.g. capital letters) which everyone repeats after the clap.
- Immediately afterwards, the student sitting on their left has to define the previous student's literacy element to which everyone claps once and then repeats the definition. There should be a constant slow clap occurring, between every clap there should be someone speaking.
- If the class feel that the student has defined incorrectly they stand up on the beat of the clap taking place. Someone else in the group explains the correct definition. Once a definition is said that everyone is happy with, everyone can sit down.
- If the class feel that the original definition is correct, another member of the group has to volunteer to give an example of the literacy element in context.
- Again, if the class agree, the game continues and another student states their name and favourite literacy element. And so the game continues as above.
- The aim is for everyone to speak. Once a student has spoken they can continue in the game but must push their chair back so that the teacher can see they have contributed.

Cross-curricular:

- Allow part of the lesson for introducing literacy subject-specific terminology.
- At the start of each topic highlight the literacy elements to look out for.
- Display the key words for your subject, a definition and an example on the classroom wall. Also give students a list—put them in the students' homework diaries.
- Instead of stating their name students could mention the name of someone who has had an impact on the subject (e.g. Churchill, Einstein, Archimedes).

Why use this strategy?

- It ensures all students speak and listen in class.
- Getting students to become physically involved through movement brings literacy to life.

- It's fun and allows students to test out their understanding of different literacy definitions.
- Drama can allow some students easier access to the curriculum.
- Excellent for revision of literacy skills.

Creativity and critical thinking – learning to learn skills:

- Learning with and from others
- Thinking

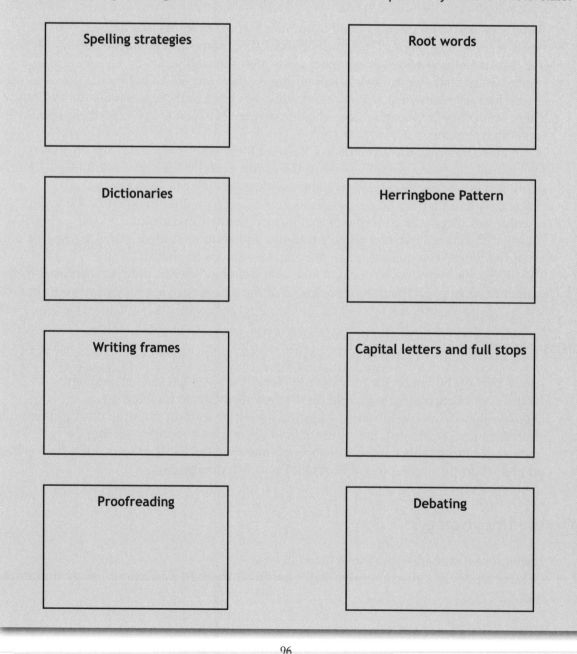

■ Literacy prompts

Some students may feel that they need some support, so let them choose a card and get them to write a definition in their own words and an example of this skill. You could do a similar activity with the rest for the class whereby they choose their own literacy skill, define it and give an example—all of these to be written on a card and then shared with the whole class before the game begins. This could be done as a warm-up activity for the whole class.

Spelling strategies	Root words
Dictionaries	Herringbone Pattern
Writing frames	Capital letters and full stops
Proofreading	Debating

40 Presentations

> *The ability to communicate is fundamental to psychological development and establishing meaningful relationships throughout life.*
>
> Alan Johnson (1950–), English politician

At some point in our lives we need to present—be it for an oral assessment, a job or at a birthday party. This strategy emphasises the skills needed when presenting.

- Arrange students into groups of four. Within their groups, students are to design a three minute presentation about the art of presenting—this can be about a topic of their choice (e.g. Genghis Khan).
- A time limit is given. Students are able to use the resources from the two resource tables—one for the subject (e.g. books on Genghis Khan) and one for presenting skills (books or items to aid in presenting).
- Students to be given roles—two presentation directors (these students are to offer opinions about the actual presentation) and two content directors (these students are to offer opinions on what material they need to include about the subject matter). However, all four students in the group will present their presentation.
- Students to present to the rest of the class.
- After each presentation, each group is to self-evaluate (see 'Presentation skills evaluation' proforma below).
- After the proforma has been filled out, it is fed back to the class. The class then offers any tips to help students develop their presentation skills.

Cross-curricular

- Good way to revise for any subject.
- Get students to come up with presentation titles.
- Have displays around the room about key speaking elements and key facts about your *who's* or *what's*—so that they can locate the literacy and subject-based information by looking around the room.

Why use this strategy?

- This strategy allows all students to learn from each others' presentations.
- Good way to revise for any subject.
- Good learning to learn technique as students need to work effectively in their groups—remember to talk about good groupwork skills as it will help students improve for next time.
- Students need to take responsibility for their learning as all students will need to speak.

Creativity and critical thinking – learning to learn skills:

- Learning with and from others
- Thinking

■ Presentation skills evaluation

Name of student: **Date:**

Topic presented	
Strengths of performance	
Targets/areas to develop	
Date targets achieved (include teacher signature)	

Keep going—you can do it!

41 Literacy chairs

Good teaching is one-fourth preparation and three-fourths theatre.

Gail Godwin (1937–), American novelist

This is another strategy to get students speaking and listening.

- Clear the desks and arrange the chairs into a circle.
- Students to sit in a circle with one student standing in the middle of the circle.
- Each student to imagine they are a speaking, reading, writing or literacy skill. Students must fill out a name badge including a brief explanation and example of that literacy skill (see badge example below).
- The game begins with the student in the middle calling out one of the literacy skills, for example, 'words'.
- All students who have chosen words as their literacy skill must stand up and introduce their explanation and example. If there are any discrepancies about definitions/examples then a class discussion occurs.
- After that, the student in the middle shouts out 'literacy chair' to which all the words students and the student in the middle have five seconds (the rest of the group counts backwards from five aloud) to change seats.
- The student who is unable to find a seat goes into the middle.
- And so the game continues. If the student in the middle shouts 'literacy' then everyone has to stand up and introduce their literacy skill, explanation and example. Then everyone changes chairs.

Cross-curricular:

- As well as asking students to state a literacy skill, ask students to repeat a fact about your subject area—you might want to open it up to the whole subject or a specific topic that you have just been studying.
- Video it. Afterwards, use the points about the subject area to develop a presentation about that topic.
- After showing the video to the class ask students to write down what they thought were the strengths of their role in the game and what they need to improve for next time—they should draw upon their learning to learn knowledge.
- For some subjects it might work to have four objects which students can relate to that subject—so they have to base their fact around the relevance of that object to the subject.

Why use this strategy?

- It encourages all students to take part.
- Listening to others is good for the self-esteem of those who are speaking as it can make them feel valued.
- Listening to others speak is an important life skill.
- It's a fun way of addressing literacy.
- This activity works well for students who are kinaesthetic learners.

Creativity and critical thinking – learning to learn skills:

- Learning with and from others
- Thinking

■ **Example of a 'literacy chairs' badge for students to fill out and wear during the game**

**Literacy skill
for literacy chairs**

Literacy skill –

Explanation –

Example –

42 Freeze-frame

This is a good strategy to reinforce speaking through drama. It's fun and works well.

- Move all the desks and chairs to the side of the classroom.
- Each student is given a badge (see example below) stating a word, reading, writing or speaking literacy skill.
- On receiving a badge, students write down an example of a literacy strategy and definition. Some of the literacy class experts could help those students who would benefit from support.
- Every student introduces their literacy skill, definition and example.
- The aim of the game is that the teacher will call out one of the literacy skills (word, speaking, writing, reading) or 'literacy' (meaning all four skills together) and students must form a group of four students containing the correct skills which have been called out. Students to share with their new group their understanding of the definition of that skill.
- Students will gain extra marks if they can make a visual image of the literacy skill (e.g. *!* seems the one that springs to mind).
- The groups that create a visual image will be able to ask the class to name another visual image literacy skill and explain it.
- And so the game continues.

Cross-curricular:

- Students combine literacy skills with facts about a topic from a subject area—so they are revising not only literacy skills but also subject knowledge.
- Hold a discussion about why these literacy skills are crucial to your subject area.
- You could ask students to connect key literacy skills with specific topics and explain why.
- Use four objects which students can relate to that subject and have them base their fact around the relevance of the object to that subject.

Why use this strategy?

- All students take part, speak and listen.
- Good for revision.
- It's a fun way of addressing literacy.
- Kinaesthetic learners will be happy as this strategy involves learning and movement married together.
- It requires students to explain their literacy skill audibly and clearly so that the rest of the class can ensure their understanding of that skill is accurate.

- Visual images will help strengthen the learning for some visual and creative learners.
- Good for developing interdependent skills.

Creativity and critical thinking – learning to learn skills:

- Learning with and from others
- Thinking

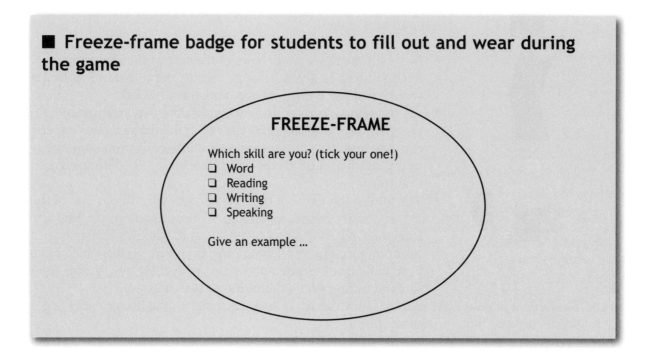

■ **Freeze-frame badge for students to fill out and wear during the game**

FREEZE-FRAME

Which skill are you? (tick your one!)
- ❑ Word
- ❑ Reading
- ❑ Writing
- ❑ Speaking

Give an example ...

43 Las Vegas - Clap and roll the dice

This is a good strategy for reinforcing speaking and listening skills.

- Push the desks to the side of the classroom and put the chairs in a circle.
- Around the walls of the room stick 40 cards about literacy skills (10 about reading, 10 about words, 10 about writing and 10 about speaking). On each card is a literacy target (e.g. using capital letters correctly), a definition (of what capital letters are) and example (a sentence showing capital letters used correctly).
- All students are divided into four teams—reading, writing, speaking or words.
- The aim of the game is for each team to collect all the cards connected with their skill from the wall and display them in the middle of the circle. However, in order to get the cards off the wall, students will need to take it in turn to roll the dice. If the dice falls on an even number the dice is passed on to the next person and nothing happens. If the dice falls on an odd number that student can collect a card from the wall (related to their team's literacy skill), place it in the middle of the circle and read it out to the group—discussion is allowed about that skill.
- The game continues until one team has won.

Cross-curricular

- Decide that different dice numbers relate to different topics—so whichever number the dice falls on, students have to state a fact about that subject-specific topic.
- As above but students answer a specific question to test their knowledge about that specific topic—you could give each group one pass card, in which case they are not penalised for not knowing the answer. Usually if they get it wrong another group automatically gets to take a card off the wall.
- Display key facts around the room—students could have done this for homework beforehand and shared these with the rest of the class. Therefore students can have a time limit to locate the correct information, e.g. five seconds.

Why use this strategy?

- Good way to revise literacy skills—speaking and listening!
- Fun!

Creativity and critical thinking - learning to learn skills:

- Learning with and from others
- Thinking

44 Let's speak all week!

> *Reading and writing float on a sea of talk.*
>
> James Britton (1908–94), educationist

Speaking is an integral part of learning. Developing speaking and listening skills will release the potential of many students. Having a 'Let's speak all week' activity is a fantastic way to ensure all students develop their speaking skills.

- In all lessons no writing is to occur for the week. The students are to focus on their speaking and listening skills. Students should complete the 'Speaking and listening self-assessment' proforma (see below).
- Start the lesson by discussing the proforma and ask students to fill out the self-assessment form.
- Teaching topics are to be covered as usual during the week, but instead of writing:
  - staff to encourage debates about topics
  - instead of writing down answers to questions get students to answer them aloud—as a competition
  - students to perform role plays (*Imagine you are in the situation of …*)
  - students take on a character and the rest of the class asks you questions about your actions
  - students to read aloud and act out scripts
  - students to imagine they are the teachers—a group of students to plan and teach a 20 minute lesson about the set topic
  - hold a 'question time'—a panel of student experts sit behind desks at the front of the classroom and answer questions
  - students to take on characters from that subject and members of the class have to find out who they are, information about their character and why they did what they did (e.g. why did they invade a country, or create long division or invent solar power).
- At the end of each task, the class re-looks at the proforma and analyses the speaking and listening which have taken place—and considers the strengths and what needs to be developed further.

Cross-curricular:

- This is a great way to revise any topic as students already have the notes and just have to creatively reflect that information in another medium apart from writing.
- Revise the literacy elements at the start of each topic.
- Remember to display the key words for your subject, definition and an example on the classroom walls. Also give students a list—put them in the students' homework diaries.
- It might be worthwhile videoing students and then watching performances on the interactive whiteboard and then assessing them.

Why use this strategy?

- The great thing about this activity is that by the end of the week all students will have spoken more than usual. The important thing is to channel their speaking and listening into ways which extend their learning—so they must develop their targets which they self-assess at the start and end of the week.
- It encourages teamwork and develops groupwork skills—it is therefore excellent for learning to learn.
- Excellent for kinaesthetic and visual learners.
- It's fun!

Creativity and critical thinking – learning to learn skills:

- Learning with and from others
- Thinking

■ Speaking and listening self-assessment form

Name:　　　　　　**Subject:**　　　　　　**Date:**

AF – Area of speaking and listening: Speaking and composing orally
1. Talk in purposeful and imaginative ways to explore ideas and feelings, using non-verbal features for clarity and effect. 3. Adapt and vary structures and vocabulary according to purpose, listeners and what is spoken about, including selecting and using the features of spoken standard English effectively.
Explain how these speaking and listening assessments relate to this subject
What do I need to improve?
Target – how will I improve?
Have I achieved my target? How?

AF - Area of speaking and listening: Listening, questioning and responding
2. Listen and respond to others, identifying main ideas, implicit meanings and viewpoints, and how these are presented. 4. Make a range of contributions when working in groups, shaping meanings through suggestions, comments and questions and drawing ideas together.
Explain how these speaking and listening assessments relate to this subject
What do I need to improve?
Target – how will I improve?
Have I achieved my target? How?

AF - Area of speaking and listening: Talking together
2. Listen and respond to others, identifying main ideas, implicit meanings and viewpoints, and how these are presented. 4. Make a range of contributions when working in groups, shaping meanings through suggestions, comments and questions and drawing ideas together.
Explain how these speaking and listening assessments relate to this subject
What do I need to improve?
Target – how will I improve?
Have I achieved my target? How?

© 2009 Amanda Sara and Crown House Publishing Ltd.

AF – Area of speaking and listening: Spoken language varieties including standard English
3. Adapt and vary structures and vocabulary according to purpose, listeners and what is spoken about, including selecting and using the features of spoken standard English effectively. 6. Identify varieties and uses of spoken language, comment on their meaning and impact and draw on these in talking to others.
Explain how these speaking and listening assessments relate to this subject
What do I need to improve?
Target – how will I improve?
Have I achieved my target? How?

AF – Area of speaking and listening: Drama skills
6. Create and sustain different roles, adapting techniques in a range of dramatic activities to explore texts, ideas and issues.
Explain how these speaking and listening assessments relate to this subject
What do I need to improve?
Target – how will I improve?
Have I achieved my target? How?

Source: Secondary National Strategy *(DfES 2007).*

Notes:

45 Diplomats

My words fly up, my thoughts remain below; Words without thoughts never to heaven go

William Shakespeare (1564–1616), English poet, from *Hamlet*, III, iii

This activity encourages students to speak up.

- Students to be put into groups of five.
- Within each group roles are issued: chair, writer, diplomat, questioner and observer.
- The aim of each group is to research a given topic for a set amount of time.
- When the time is up, the diplomat leaves that group and imparts the knowledge learnt to the next group and so on.
- The winner is the group whose diplomat manages to gain the diplomatic car number plates for their original group. In return for the diplomat imparting their knowledge, the group they join shares their original knowledge with the diplomat. However, each group ranks each one of the diplomats out of three: one mark for eye contact, one mark for imparting knowledge and one mark for making the group feel comfortable with the knowledge—confidence.
- The rules are as follows:
  - The diplomat is allowed diplomatic immunity from one group's questions—students to use the 'diplomatic immunity card'.
  - The diplomat can ask the embassy (teacher) for help once.
  - The diplomat has to travel to each group and impart the knowledge they've learnt so the other groups feel secure with their knowledge. If the diplomat is uncertain about teaching a group they can use the above resources.
- The roles within the group are to ensure that everyone is on task. The chair is to ensure that learning is taking place and everyone is fulfilling their role. The writer is minuting the notes. The diplomat imparts their original knowledge to all the groups. The questioner is to ask at least five questions to each diplomat to ensure that their group has a clear understanding and the observer is to make notes about everyone in their group— their strengths and areas to develop (see 'Observer' proforma below).
- When all the diplomats have finished, marks are added up and the highest winning diplomat gains his/her diplomatic number plates. The diplomatic number plate consists of three numbers (these identify the country) followed by a D or X and then three more numbers (these identify the vehicle within the country).
- Remember to have the observers feed back to their groups about the learning, so that students can look for ways to get even better at learning!

Cross-curricular:

- Ideal for students to learn procedures or rules, for example in PE.
- Ideal for all subjects to test understanding and as a strategy for revising.
- Good development of students' learning to learn skills
- You could, at the start of the game, have a couple of students to be known as the experts of that literacy and subject area and they are to ensure that all students are up to speed with specific literacy skills and subject knowledge introduced—they become sub-teachers.

Why use this strategy?

- Develops all students' speaking and listening skills.
- This activity encourages teamwork and develops groupwork skills—and is excellent for learning to learn.
- It's fun and gives students a taste of diplomatic life!
- It encourages students to take responsibility for their learning and encouraging others to learn as well.
- The teacher is available to observe rather than lead.

Creativity and critical thinking – learning to learn skills:

- Learning with and from others
- Thinking

■ Observer observation sheet

	Name of student	Strengths of performance	Areas to develop
Chair			
Writer			
Diplomat			
Questioner			
Observer			

46 Rise from the dead – Become a specialist of your subject

> *Adults are so familiar with [speaking and listening] ... we rarely acknowledge them as complex, learnt skills, except when visiting a foreign country.*
>
> Colin Grigg, writer

- Teacher-led discussion about the skills needed for presenting:
  - audibility
  - eye contact
  - keep to the point
  - relevance
  - structure—introduction, middle and conclusion
  - smile
  - remember the audience doesn't know your speech, so they won't know if you've made a mistake
  - be confident—don't giggle unless it's part of the presentation
  - relax and put the audience at ease.
- Students, in pairs, to be given a card on which is the name of a character/person/ subject/symbol (e.g. fractions in Maths). This is to be kept a secret from the rest of the class as their role will be to guess the subject.
- In pairs, students to plan how to present their topic to the rest of the class. They are allowed to make visual props. However, their focus should be on their dialogue and acting.
- Time limit to be set.
- Pairs to present to the rest of class and students to guess the subject.
- If a student thinks they know who/what is being acted, they shout out the word 'speaking' and then give the answer.
- And so the game continues.
- After each presentation, pairs to self-evaluate and class to offer tips to help them with their speaking skills.

Cross-curricular:

- Good way to revise for any subject.
- It gets students to come up with who or what is to be acted out.
- Have displays around the classroom about key speaking elements and key facts about your *who's* or *what's*, so that students can locate the literacy and subject-based information by looking around the room.
- You could have a resource table which will help students put together their sketch.
- Discussion to be held after each performance about the audience's listening skills—their strengths and areas to develop.

Why use this strategy?

- Students need to take responsibility for their learning through speaking and listening and this game promotes that.
- Good revision tool to test prior learning.
- Good learning to learn exercise as students need to work effectively in their pairs—remember to talk about good paired work as it will help students improve for next time.
- It's a game, so hopefully it is fun!

Creativity and critical thinking - learning to learn skills:

- Learning with and from others
- Thinking

47 Questions – Open and closed

> *Effective communication and language skills are fundamental to young people's learning, developing social skills and fulfilling their potential.*
>
> **Ed Balls (1967–), British politician**

Closed questions have *yes* or *no* answers, a single word or short phrase as the answer. Examples of closed questions are: What day is it? Do you have a brother? Is it raining? Usually they are easy-to-answer questions which require a simple fact.

Open questions tend to begin with: *what, why, how* or *describe*. They require longer answers and usually ask for you to express your opinions and feelings. As a result you gain control of the conversation and can talk in greater depth and give examples (e.g. *generally it is thought that …, but I think …, because …, I remember when …, so this is why …*). Examples of open questions are: What do you think the next Olympics will be like? Why do you want to compete in the next Olympics? How will you go about training for the next Olympics?

- Class brainstorm the merits of open and closed questions.
- Students to work in pairs to analyse a text—the literacy focus is on open and closed questions.
- Individually, students to write two closed questions about the text and five open questions.
- In pairs, students to ask each other closed questions and then open questions. Students to use connectives to extend their answers (see Strategy 7). Students should try to speak for a minimum of 15 seconds in their answer to each open question.
- Teacher collects in all the questions and asks individual students open questions about the text.
- Students must try to break the 15 second talking barrier—whoever can talk the longest (no longer than three minutes) is crowned the winner. However, students must talk sense!
- And so the game continues.

Cross-curricular:

- All subjects require conversation and this promotes students talking but in the depth required, rather than the usual one word answer.
- Try to get students answering a variety of open and closed questions in your lessons—get them to identify which is an open question and which is a closed question.
- Easy to promote in form times—ask a couple of open and closed questions each morning or even better nominate two students to be your daily open and closed question experts.

Why use this strategy?

- It encourages students to think about what they are saying and talk in greater depth.
- It's a game, so has a competitive element to it. Hopefully this will motivate students to transfer these skills from one class to the next.
- It encourages teamwork and develops groupwork skills—it is therefore excellent for learning to learn.
- It's a good way of revising your subject.
- It gets students thinking.

Creativity and critical thinking – learning to learn skills:

- Learning with and from others
- Thinking

48 Weather corners

> *Fall seven times, stand up eight.*
> Japanese proverb

This is another strategy to promote speaking and listening.

- Clear all desks to the side of the room or ideally use the library.

- In three of the corners of the room put up signs:
  CORNER 1: YELLOW SUN – *Literacy is improving in this subject.*
  CORNER 2: GREY RAIN – *I'm not sure whether literacy is happening.*
  CORNER 3: BLACK THUNDER – *Literacy is not developing in my subject.*
- Students are given two minutes to reflect upon their literacy development in that subject. On a card (see proforma below) they self-evaluate their literacy development.
- Students to share their written proformas with neighbours—two minute discussion time given.
- Students then asked to stand in corner 1, 2 or 3, whichever they feel reflects their evaluation of their literacy development.
- Each student given a number for that corner (so you might have a corner 1 number 1 student or corner 2 number 1 student and so on).
- Staff member then shuffles a pack of cards (on the cards are corner numbers and student numbers).
- When a student's number is called out, they read out their review of their literacy level.
- The rest of the class has two minutes within their groups to come up with two strategies that will help that student improve and develop. Each corner will need to appoint a spokesperson to feed back to the class.
- The game continues until all the cards are removed from the deck.

Cross-curricular:

- Students to evaluate topics in that subject area—what they feel they have learnt well and what they need to work on.
- Students could also review learning to learn skills developed in that subject and how they could ensure they continue to blossom.
- Teachers could pick specific topics and have class expert judges who ask students questions about those topics to test their understanding of those areas.
- Student expert judges could present objects and ask students to explain their relevance to the topic—the response would show how much they understood and revised that topic.

Why use this strategy?

- It encourages speaking and listening skills, so makes the student who is talking feel valued—the importance of this must be emphasised to the class beforehand.
- Inclusive—all students will share their self-reviews with the class (if you think this would not be suitable for all students then ask them to share their feedback with teaching assistants or experts and get feedback from them instead).
- Enjoyable!
- It encourages teamwork.
- It's gives students the chance to hear other students' views about them, so that they all know that everyone has to develop—they are all learners.

Creativity and critical thinking – learning to learn skills:

- Learning with and from others
- Thinking

■ **Displays for the three corners**

CORNER 1: YELLOW SUN

Literacy is improving in this subject.

CORNER 2: GREY RAIN

I'm not sure whether literacy is happening.

CORNER 3: BLACK THUNDER

Literacy is not developing in my subject.

■ Literacy self-evaluation

Name:
Subject:
Term and year:

Tick one of the following:

❏ *CORNER 1: YELLOW SUN* – *Literacy is improving in this subject.*

❏ *CORNER 2: GREY RAIN* – *I'm not sure whether literacy is happening.*

❏ *CORNER 3: BLACK THUNDER* – *Literacy is not developing in my subject.*

Explain your choice:

Literacy areas covered in that subject:

What can I do to help myself develop in literacy in this subject (write down two strategies)?

1.

2.

Strategies which the other corners suggest:

•

•

•

•

49 Voicemail!

> *All children are artists.*
> Pablo Picasso (1881–1973), artist

The class forms a circle and a message is passed around the circle and added to. This is a good strategy to promote speaking and listening.

- Clear the desks and arrange the chairs into a circle.
- Students to sit in a circle.
- Invite a student to begin. They tell a message to the student sitting next to them. The message must explain a literacy skill—state it, explain it and example it!
- The student who receives the message must repeat it in its entirety and add their own literacy skill—state it, explain it and example it! And so on. The message is passed around the circle with each additional student adding their message.
- If a student in the circle feels that one of the previous students has defined a skill incorrectly they shout 'operator' and the student who defined the skill incorrectly is given a phone bill. The game is frozen and the class as a whole examine the 'state it, explain it and example it!' of the literacy skill given.
- If a student shouts 'operator' and they are correct, they are handed the CEO (Chief Executive Officer) badge—they become one of the experts.
- Once everyone in the circle has messaged, a class discussion is held about the messages.

Cross-curricular

- At the start of each topic allow a couple of students to be known as the experts of that literacy area and they are to ensure that all students are up to speed with the specific literacy skills being developed. At the start of the lesson allow your experts to reintroduce literacy subject-specific terminology.
- Quick revision of literacy elements in topics to look out for.
- Remember to display the key words for your subject, definition and an example on the classroom walls. Also give students a list—put them in the students' homework diaries.
- Instead of saying 'operator' students could mention a key topic from that subject.
- Work in smaller groups and have an expert in each group.
- It might be worthwhile getting students to write down a literacy skill—state it, explain it and example it!—before game begins. Some students might benefit from working in pairs to achieve this. Pair up an expert with a student who would benefit from their expertise.

Why use this strategy?

- It's fun and allows students to test out their understanding of different literacy definitions, while developing their speaking and literacy abilities.
- It encourages teamwork and develops groupwork skills—it is therefore excellent for learning to learn.
- Suits learners who like to be active.
- Drama can allow some students easier access to the curriculum.
- It's a good way of revising literacy skills across the curriculum.

Creativity and critical thinking – learning to learn skills:

- Learning with and from others
- Thinking

■ Literacy prompts for Voicemail!

Some students might benefit from completing the first card before beginning the game. It might be worthwhile pairing up literacy experts with those students in need of additional support.

The additional cards are to add to the fun factor—cards should be put in the middle of the circle so that if students need to distribute them they can reach in and get one. Enjoy!

A literacy skill – state it, explain it and example it!

Literacy skill –
Explain skill –
Example –

CEO

Congratulations! You have just been promoted to CEO (Chief Executive Officer). People work for many years to achieve this status—you've achieved it today! Well done!

Operator

There is a possibility that someone has made a mistake with their ... literacy skill—state it, explain it and example it! Who is it and can we correct it?

Phone bill

You have incorrectly explained your ... literacy skill—state it, explain it and example it! This will need to be resolved immediately.

---

50 United students!

> *To teach is to learn twice.*
>
> Joseph Joubert (1754–1824), French essayist

This strategy encourages students to talk in the depth required, rather than the usual one word answers which can often happen when presenting!

- Students to be divided into groups of three.
- Each group is given a sub-topic of the topic being studied at present to discuss in their group for a timed period.
- When the time is up, students form new groups with different students.
- Each student feeds back to their new group about the original topic they have just discussed—everyone in the group must talk for a minimum of one minute about the topic.
- Anyone who does not talk for a minute will have to present the whole group's discussion to the whole class!
- Like diplomats (see Strategy 45), students should make eye contact and ensure their group understands and feels comfortable with their new found knowledge. All students to grade all talkers (see 'Speaking evaluation' proforma below).
- End with a class discussion about speaking skills.

Cross-curricular:

- Easy strategy to do in any subject—though you might want to make the groups smaller unless you have the space.
- You could ask students to ask open and closed questions after each student has presented!

Why use this strategy?

- Inclusive—all students have to speak and listen!
- Students need to take responsibility for their learning as they will need to express understanding to the group.
- It encourages students to think about what they are saying and talk in greater depth.
- It's a game, so hopefully it is fun!
- It encourages teamwork and develops groupwork skills—it is therefore excellent for learning to learn.
- It's a good way of revising a topic.

Creativity and critical thinking - learning to learn skills:

- Learning with and from others
- Thinking

■ United students! – Speaking evaluation

Name of speaker:	Was it loud enough?	Did they smile and make you feel at ease?	Eye contact?	Enough depth to their speech?	Targets?

Chapter 3
Whole School Strategies

What follows is a range of strategies which have been used across numerous schools and academies to develop some of the key areas of literacy.

Effective literacy

Acquiring literacy is an empowering process, enabling millions to enjoy access to knowledge and information which broadens horizons.

Kofi Annan (1938–), former Secretary General of the United Nations, awarded the Nobel Peace Prize

When introducing literacy to your school it is worthwhile clarifying the following points among your staff so that everyone is starting from a common ground: What is literacy? Why do we want it? Why do we need it as a whole school approach?

It is important to ensure that staff have a clear understanding of which literacy strategies have been trialled and achieved within your school, what your school literacy vision is and what that will entail.

Literacy impacts on the results of all subjects, so it is important that every staff member takes ownership of its development. Ideally, literacy should be seen as a vital part of the school culture. The ultimate aim is for staff to embrace literacy as part of their school ethos. If this is to occur, it is important that staff receive the necessary training, time and resources so they can develop literacy in your school. In addition, it is crucial that literacy has a whole school focus and that high literacy expectations cascade from staff and students.

It would be advisable to set up working parties which meet regularly to ensure that literacy aims set by the faculties and pastoral teams are on target and that exemplary materials are available. Furthermore, use a buddy system whereby staff can receive support from other colleagues to develop and deliver literacy-focused teaching.

In order for literacy to have a whole school focus, the following areas need to be addressed:

- Working parties created with pastoral and faculty leaders setting clear aims and gathering exemplary materials.
- Training days on the four key aspects of literacy—words, reading, writing and speaking.
- Whole school, faculty and pastoral literacy policies.
- Greater use of ICT and the library.
- Parents' involvement in the development of their child's literacy.
- Lesson observation to ensure the literacy element is evident and progressive.
- Literacy assessment, monitoring, evaluations, targets and action plans.
- Schemes of learning to have an evident literacy focus.
- Literacy skills and vocabulary written in students' homework diaries.
- 'Word of the week' for the whole school.
- Buddy system whereby older pupils listen to younger pupils read in form time.

It is also worthwhile considering the following to further develop literacy skills:

- Booster classes.
- Literacy summer school.
- Literacy breakfast clubs.
- Additional literacy homework packs.
- Grammar lessons once a week for all (a contentious issue but this would be in addition to the literacy focus taught through the units).
- Mind exercises to keep minds sharp.
- Developing learning to learn skills and attitudes to develop the skills and attitudes needed to ensure students are better literacy learners.

When looking at the key literacy areas to develop—words, reading, writing and speaking—it is worth considering the following:

Reading:
- Parents and children reading together
- Reading in registration
- Buddy reading with older years in lunchtimes
- Reading for meaning using DARTS (Directed Activities Related To Texts) approach
- Active research

Writing:
- Writing frames and conventions
- Modelling – sequence and variety
- Sentence starters
- Connectives

Speaking:
- Greater channelled speaking in form time (see p. 133)
- 'Talk, talk, talk' week
- Get students talking/involved in assemblies
- Student buddy talking system
- Increased staff confidence in student talk

Words:
- Spelling
- Vocabulary
- Roots

However, before developing your literacy action plan, it is worth considering the following questions: What do we need to do? How will we achieve this? What will be our action plan and how will we measure our success?

Leading cross-curricular literacy, training staff, monitoring outcomes and assessment

> *No matter how thoroughly a person may have learned the Greek alphabet, he will never be in a condition to repeat it backwards without further training.*
>
> Hermann Ebbinghaus (1850–1909), German psychologist

Literacy is a constant and ongoing challenge we are all trying to address. We need to immerse literacy into the everyday culture of the school, ensure that we have cross-curricular working parties, train staff appropriately and continually monitor and assess.

As a school you want to lead in the following areas:

- Training – ensure all staff and departments are given the training that meets their needs.
- Use data – ensure all staff use the data supplied to build up an accurate profile of each student so that you can cater for their needs.
- Monitor impact and give feedback.
- Time – ensure staff have enough time to get the job done well.
- Teacher ownership – ensure staff feel they have ownership of literacy development.

If we look closer at training needs, perhaps the best way forward is to consider the following:

- Bring in experts.
- Allow research teachers to be experts.
- Student voice – student team of literacy experts.
- *The Literacy Toolkit* in each room.
- All lesson starters and plenaries to be literacy based.
- Homework diaries to include rules about vocabulary, text types, connectives and sentence starters.

It is then worth considering monitoring for impact and thinking about ways to assess:

- Student self-evaluation of literacy.
- Staff evaluation of literacy.
- Action plans.
- Shared analysis of data.
- Regular assessment and monitoring.
- Priorities/targets met for each subject area.

In addition, the following questions need to be discussed:

- What do we need to do as a school to progress further with literacy?
- What do my faculty/pastoral team need to do to progress further?
- What do I need to do to ensure that my teaching shows literacy progression?

Remember, that although it might seem quite daunting if you have fun with literacy things will progress positively.

Below are the proformas for the 'Whole school literacy focus' strategy, enabling the literacy coordinator and the senior leadership team to have a clear focus of what is being covered in each departmental team; the 'Student literacy self-evaluation' strategy, in order that we can see students' perceptions of their literacy habits; the 'Student voice – Roles for students' strategy, so that students can highlight literacy through the student voice (teachers can decide whether students or teachers issue roles); and finally, included by popular demand, a list of connectives students should be using to advance their literacy skills. It might be helpful to put a copy of this in the students' homework diaries.

■ Whole school literacy focus

Subject	Literacy objective	Action to achieve objective	Time frame to be achieved by	By whom	Evidence of success	Achieved
English						
Maths						
Science						
Art						
D&T						
Music						
Drama						
History						
RE						
Geography						
PE						
MFL						

■ Student literacy self-evaluation

Name:

Target	Where am I now? Tick OK or write challenge with this area of literacy.	Review date	Progress
Capital letters			
Full stops			
Commas			
Paragraphs			
Speech			
Question marks			
Exclamation marks			
Colons			
Semi-colons			
Conjunctions			
Planning			
Homophones			
Proofreading			
Skimming and scanning			
Using evidence			
Using subject-specific vocabulary			
Using the correct writing for different text types			
Speaking			
Listening			

■ Student voice – Roles for students

Either students or teachers can issue roles, but it is helpful for students to cover these areas in order to develop their literacy skills, as well as adding to the fun factor!

The chair Ensures everyone is contributing—speaking and listening in an orderly manner.	**Welcome spokesperson** Welcomes anyone who enters the room and explains what the class are learning and what the literacy focus is.
Mr/Miss Congratulations Praises *two* students who have worked well and shown an understanding of the literacy focus.	**Literacy coordinator** Locates the best *two* examples of understanding of the literacy focus.
Mr/Miss Assessment Uses the level descriptors to work out the standard of work.	**Mr/Miss Learning to learn** Locates *two* examples of students learning well.
Mr/Miss Questionnaire Must ask *four* open questions and *two* closed questions.	**Mr/Miss Emotional well-being** Explains what emotions have been used today and how that helped the class.

■ Connectives students should be using

- ➤ However
- ➤ Although
- ➤ But
- ➤ Yet
- ➤ Then again
- ➤ Still
- ➤ Nevertheless
- ➤ Nonetheless
- ➤ Whereas
- ➤ On the other hand
- ➤ Conversely
- ➤ Similarly
- ➤ Also
- ➤ In the same way
- ➤ Correspondingly
- ➤ Equally
- ➤ Furthermore
- ➤ Additionally
- ➤ In addition
- ➤ Besides
- ➤ Plus

All staff involvement in developing literacy across the curriculum

There is nothing training cannot do.

Mark Twain (1835–1910), American writer

The questions your team need to answer and discuss are as follows:

- Why is literacy across the curriculum important?
- What are the problems for teachers as a whole?
- What are the pitfalls for you as an individual teacher?
- What do you think the literacy requirements of your subject are?
- How can you meet them?

The ingredients for literacy success at your school will probably include some of the following:

- Literacy to be integrated into teaching and learning as a whole school approach.
- Provide time, resources, expert regular training sessions and administrative support for staff.
- Involve parents, pupils and governors in the literacy process.
- Be prepared to address the following issues: funding, literacy knowledge and staff confidence in literacy, pupil data, maintaining momentum, poor staff morale and a lack of understanding of primary practice.

Each staff member needs to be reminded that the four key aspects to literacy across the curriculum are: words, reading, writing and talking. It would be beneficial to gather a group of enthusiasts who could develop a staff-owned development plan and help other staff to create SMART (Specific, Measurable, Achievable, Realistic, Timebound) targets. Furthermore, some departmental meeting time should be set aside to share good practice and modelling.

In addition, time to create literacy planning strategies would be received well by staff, as well as time to monitor, evaluate and assess literacy development and the creation of a buddy system for staff so that everyone has a literacy critical friend. Another strategy that works well is to show videos of primary practice, run literacy Insets, create literacy newsletters and competitions for staff and pupils, get your students involved and use the student voice to develop literacy in your school.

It is important that we recognise the literacy demands of each subject. Each faculty will need to:

- Update schemes of learning to include literacy.
- Create a literacy policy stating which areas of literacy will be addressed.
- Include subject-specific displays of words—subject-specific word of the week.
- Introduce lesson observations to reinforce literacy.
- Build on Year 6 work.

It is important to get all staff involved in building a literacy community within your school. Remember that newly qualified teachers are up to date with the latest ideas and it is worthwhile channelling their energies and enthusiasm into literacy.

Websites such as www.readingconnects.org.uk have some great ideas that will help improve reading and literacy—have a look!

As a whole school it might be helpful to create the following:

- A strong foundation—a working party of enthusiasts for literacy, including a senior manager to share good practice. Bring in an expert.
- Literacy half-termly competitions for staff and pupils (see example below).
- Literacy newsletter focusing on the chosen aspect, such as spelling (see example below).

■ Literacy across the curriculum

Below is this term's literacy competition. Prizes will be awarded for the best entry at Key Stage 3 and the best entry at Key Stage 4. Certificates will be issued to all those who take part.

To take part in this term's competition students will need to complete the following:

Task 1 - Contradictions

The following are contradictions; they are words that do not mean what they say, e.g.

> Abbreviation - why is it such a long word?
> Monosyllabic - why does it have five syllables?

Now find five words which are also contradictions.

Task 2 - Pleonasties

This term refers to the use of more words than are needed (usually two) to explain an idea, e.g.

> end result
> empty space

Now write five other pleonasties.

Task 3

Write a shape poem including contradictions and pleonasties.

Winners will be announced in assembly before the end of this term. Please give your entries to the Literacy Coordinator before the half-term.

■ Literacy Newsletter

Welcome to the Literacy Newsletter—out every term! This issue aims to promote a set of strategies for teaching students how to learn and retain spellings.

How do we address spelling?

It doesn't matter what subject you teach, spelling is an issue for many students. So what can we do to improve this?

The following techniques can help: sounds, syllables, visual memory, sight, analogy, etymology, words within words, say it, word families, mnemonics and spelling rules. OK, so how do we use these?

➤ The following is a list of words which are often misspelt. Ask students to come up with strategies that might help another student who is misspelling them.

question	said	diary	where
does	because	there	February
remember	socks	liquefy	conscientious
definite	their	were	

➤ Share spelling strategies with students:
  – Remember to stare, conceal, note down, confirm
  – Use the spelling rules
  – Say it out loud (Mon-day)
  – Look at the words inside words (conscience—con-science)
  – Reduce words into sounds (r-o-o-m)
  – Put words into syllables (re-mem-ber)
  – Add affixes (un+happy)
  – Encourage the use of mnemonic (said—I said)
  – Remember to use the same family (dissect, dissection, dissecting)
  – Etymology (bi+lingual = two + languages)
  – Remember to use analogy (hot, fire, cold, ice)
  – Use word webs (the first and the last words in each list are starting points for a new list)

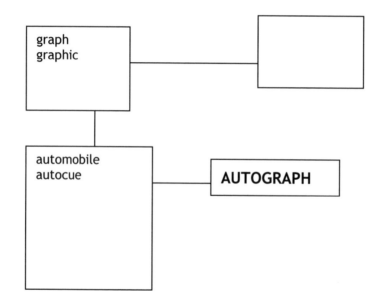

Literacy development across the school
  ➤ Any subject can use these strategies and it will help students think about the meaning of words due to their similarities with other words and improve spelling.
  ➤ Encourage students to use the spellcheck on computers.
  ➤ Display and give out a subject-specific vocabulary list—can this be added to school home-work planners?
  ➤ Ensure that every classroom has subject-specific dictionaries.
  ➤ Make word and definition card boxes.
  ➤ Students create a booklet containing an alphabetical list of keywords from a unit of work. Leave a blank line alongside each. Produce a separate sheet of definitions. At the end of each lesson stress two or three keywords. Students should find those keywords in their own glossary and put the correct definitions next to each.

If you would like any more information, please see your Literacy Coordinator.

Using ICT and media to develop students' literacy

We must prepare young people for living in a world of powerful images, words and sounds.

UNESCO (1982)

Today's definition of literacy is more than reading and writing. In order to be functionally literate in our media saturated world, children and young people—in fact all of us—have to be able to read messages that daily inform us, entertain us and sell to us. As the Internet becomes a fact of life, the critical thinking skills that help young people navigate through traditional media are even more important.

Media Awareness Network (www.media-awareness.ca/english/teachers/ media_literacy/why_teach_media_liter.cfm)

Literacy now encompasses the world of media literacy—a world which for most children is with them from a young age, more so than the world of books which for many teachers were with us in our younger years. To begin, why don't you ask your class to complete the popular culture questionnaire (below) about reading texts, including media texts. I'm sure you will find the results informative.

Ways to use ICT and media texts in your literacy teaching include:

- SPG (spelling, punctuation, grammar)
- Writing frames (the See/Hide button on a standard toolbar)
- Visiting *Blockbusters* at www.itv.com/games/tvgames/blockbusters/
- Using audio recording on a PC
- Using verbal comments on a PC (for written texts and pictures)
- Using free Microsoft Reader software to read e-books and link to dictionary and thesaurus pages
- Using a digital movie maker to make movies, write scripts, add subtitles, etc.
- Creating blogs and discussion rooms for staff and pupils
- Watching DVDs with subtitles
- Using the internet for podcasts
- Making library materials available to parents online so they can track their child's reading habits
- Using the Word of the Day website at www.wordofthedaywebsite.com
- Using the Kar2ouche composer to improve writing
- Using screen capture tools such as Screen Flash
- Using mind mapping software like FreeMind and OpenMind
- Moodle
- Virtual learning
- Using Renaissance Learning software to personalise learning for accelerated readers—students read books and then complete quizzes.

■ Questionnaire – Popular culture

Name: **Form:**

Please tick appropriate box and add comments if necessary.

1) What do you read?

   ❑ books
   ❑ comics
   ❑ magazines
   ❑ newspapers
   ❑ leaflets
   ❑ school textbooks
   ❑ posters
   ❑ internet
   ❑ Other, please explain:_____

   _____

   Additional comments: _____

   _____

2) How would you define reading?

3) How much reading do you do each week?

	Book:	Reading images:
0 minutes		
1-15 minutes		
15-30 minutes		
30-45 minutes		
45-60 minutes		
1-1½ hours		
1½-2 hours		
2 hours plus		

4) What do you think is meant by the phrase *reading images*?

5) Do you think reading images of the written text helps your understanding?
   ❑ Yes
   ❑ No

6) Why?

7) Do you think that talking about visual texts helps you understand written text?

8) What do you enjoy reading?

9) What/who encourages children to read?

10) Do you think that reading the same text in different formats helps (i.e. reading a book, comic and watching a video all of the same text)?

The role of oracy in form time to transform literacy

Words are the voice of the heart.

Confucius (551–479 BC), Chinese thinker and social philosopher

Secondary schools receive feedback from pupils and staff asking for ways to help pupils become more articulate. The four key elements to literacy across the curriculum are words, reading, writing and talking. To tackle oracy pupils need to be given the following further opportunities:

- to explain, justify and describe what they learn from their lessons
- to explore, discuss and develop their ideas
- to discuss effectively and make outcomes of discussion clear.

Oracy is an integral part of literacy. Research highlights that there is a definite link between speaking and listening and thinking. Speaking and listening is a powerful tool in generating new learning; therefore, oracy is one of the keys to unlocking the potential of all students and an essential route to raising achievement. In the National Literacy Strategy the emphasis upon speaking is stressed. Even at GCSE level, 20% of the total mark is awarded for speaking and listening, and likewise the Every Child Matters agenda highlights the importance of speaking and listening as the link between enjoyment and achievement.

So, as well as addressing oracy in subject areas I feel form time is the perfect opportunity to develop speaking and listening. I introduced a public speaking unit which was led by form tutors during tutorial periods to give pupils opportunities to develop their confidence and effectiveness in speaking in a secure environment. The innovation, across all years of a secondary school, highlighted the importance of delivery during a speech and how to connect emotionally with the audience through voice, eye contact and body language, and furthermore, to structure a speech to allow the audience to follow the arguments clearly. The innovation was a success.

I introduced the innovation at a mixed secondary school in West London with 1,200 pupils aged between 11 and 16 years. The school is a specialist technology college. The school population is ethnically diverse: almost all students come from minority ethnic groups, predominately of Indian or Pakistani heritage and most have English as a second language. The proportion of students with learning difficulties and disabilities is above the national average, as are levels of social and economic deprivation.

The research took a qualitative approach although some quantitative data collection methods were used at the start and end of the project. Questionnaires and semi-structured interviews with pupils were used over the period of a term.

As well as addressing speaking, the innovation focused on responsiveness and learning with others—an important learning to learn attitude and skill. Each lesson began with an introduction about the importance of public speaking, followed by a fun starter, such as pupils talking for 30 seconds about a given subject, picture or object.

This was followed by a development activity in which the teacher introduced an area of public speaking, such as confidence. This was followed by group discussion and presentations.

Finally a plenary was held during which the pupils were given a booklet summarising each 'lesson'.

To maximise the efficiency of the innovation, the programme was covered by all pupils in tutorial time lasting for one hour every week for one term.

Form tutors were fully trained prior to the commencement of the project to ensure that the training sessions were delivered successfully. In accordance with feedback from the pupils, the form tutors were assisted in the delivery of the innovation by the form's debater.

Written feedback from staff and pupils at the end of the innovation showed that the programme had a positive impact upon the pupils. Two Key Stage 3 English classes (a Year 9/Set 2 and a Year 7/Set 4) were tested for speaking and listening levels at the start and end of the innovation. All En1 levels remained constant or improved by one level. In the Year 7 class En1 levels improved by 100%, 80% by one level and 20% by two levels. In the Year 9 class 30% stayed at the same level and 70% rose by one level.

It was also noted by staff that generally pupils appeared more confident at speaking effectively in lessons.

It is clear therefore that the innovation worked. It is particularly important to note that public speaking was an area which pupils had identified as one in which they needed development. As a consequence the students were much more receptive to the innovation, which I believe was a factor in its success.

So what did those involved think, I hear you ask? Well, the comments included:

I felt that talking in front of the class gave me more confidence and you could see others getting braver with each new week as it was fun and safe.

Year 7 girl

I think the public speaking unit was a good way to help pupils express our views and learn from others' viewpoints. Also, I think that the explanations and tips about public speaking improved my confidence in this. I'm just glad that I suggested that talking was something that would help my English.

Year 9 boy

It made form time a joy! I was sceptical but now, much to my amazement, my tutees structure their discussions!

Year 10 form tutor

So, how do we do that?

This is what we used:

■ Suggested teacher notes

Public speaking – Form time

6 weeks

Learning objectives:

Must recognise the impact of delivery on a speech.
Should recognise the necessity of structure when giving a speech.
Could recognise the importance of body language.

Learning to learn:

Responsiveness.
Learning with others.

	Intro/notes/ resources	Starter	Development	Plenary
Week 1	Introduce the importance of public speaking	Each pupil to talk for 30 seconds about a typical day/week at school OR If you could be anyone who would it be and why? However, the pupil is not allowed to say 'em' or pause for longer than three seconds. See who can talk for the longest	Ask pupils about their confidence levels at public speaking Class discussion – Top 10 ideas for speaking in public Pupils to present a one minute talk about something they feel passionate about (e.g. why Manchester United are the best football team)	Questions: What have you learnt about public speaking? What are the top tips for public speaking? How do you think you will use what has been covered today to improve your public speaking?
Week 2		Teacher to state five statements. After each statement pupils to stand on either side of the room—believe or not believe. Each pupil to say why they believe/ don't believe in the following statements: 1. Rap music should be banned 2. Girls are just as good as boys at sports 3. Husbands should be allowed to have more than one wife 4. Britain should get rid of the royal family 5. Children under 16 years should not be given chocolate	Class discussion – Top 10 ideas for handling questions and answers Five pupils to sit at the front of the class and take questions about their lives as a character they have chosen (e.g. the Prime Minister, Prince Charles, Ryan Giggs, Britney Spears). Try to change the panel every five minutes	What are the top tips for handling questions and answers? What did you do well today? What must you do to improve next time?

135

	Intro/notes/ resources	Starter	Development	Plenary
Week 3		Pupils put in groups of three. One pupil from the group tells a story from their childhood. Each member of the group repeats the story to the class. The class have to ask questions about the incident to work out whose childhood it is from. Each group to perform	Class discussion – Top 10 ideas for overcoming nerves Impromptu speaking – In pairs pupils called to the front of the class to discuss one of the following individually: • Is there such a thing as a superior race? • Health, wealth, or love—which matters to you and why? • Men are from Mars; women are from Venus. What are your thoughts? • Do you think that space travel is a good idea? Will you go and why? • Do you think it is fair to have seven wives? Why? • Do you think the Queen should step down and Prince Charles should be King? Why? • The film *Alive* was the true story of a rugby team whose aeroplane crashed into the Andes and the only way for them to survive was through cannibalism— what are your thoughts? • Are schools responsible for teaching good manners? • Do you think that parents should be punished for their children's hooliganism? • Do you think there is too much emphasis on physical appearance? Why? • Should Prince Harry be sent to the front line? Why?	Why is it important to overcome nerves? What general things can you do to overcome nerves?
Week 4	Pictures of people	Teacher to show class pictures. Pupils to explain the thoughts of the characters in the pictures	Class discussion – Five things not to do when public speaking Pupils to present a one minute talk about public speaking	What did the class as a whole do well at today? What do you think the class should try to improve?

	Intro/notes/ resources	Starter	Development	Plenary
Week 5	Any three objects	Teacher to present to class three objects. Teacher to begin a story. 'Once upon a time ...' story to continue going around the class— each pupil to say at least a sentence including one of the three objects	Class discussion – How to run a debate Classes to prepare debate: • Year 7 – This house believes that footballers are paid too much money • Year 8 – This house believes that global warming is both a corporate and personal responsibility • Year 9 – This house believes that hip pop and violence are closely related • Year 10 – This house believes that police officers should carry guns	Why are debates useful?
Week 6	Random objects	One pupil to stand at the front of the class and be an archaeologist expert with an ancient item (e.g. keys). Pupil to attempt to convince the class that the item is an ancient object through description (e.g. earrings worn by Cleopatra)	Class discussion – Recap top ten ideas for speaking in public Classes to have debate prepared last week: • Year 7 –This house believes that footballers are paid too much money • Year 8 – This house believes that global warming is both a corporate and personal responsibility • Year 9 – This house believes that hip pop and violence are closely related • Year 10 – This house believes that police officers should carry guns	Evaluation: What have you learnt over the course of this unit? What skills have you developed? What areas do you still need to work on? What are you going to do to continue to develop those skills?

■ Suggested Year 11 teacher notes

Public speaking – Form time

6 weeks

Learning objectives:

Must recognise the impact of delivery on a speech.
Should recognise the necessity of structure when giving a speech.
Could recognise the importance of body language.

Learning to learn:

Responsiveness.
Learning with others.

	Intro/ notes/ resources	Starter	Development	Plenary
Week 1	Introduce the importance of public speaking, especially in interviews	Each pupil to stand at the front of the class and read out a nursery rhyme with expression	Ask pupils about their confidence levels at public speaking Class discussion – Top ten ideas for speaking in public Five pupils to sit at the front of the class and answer interview questions about their lives as the character they have chosen (e.g. the Prime Minister, Prince Charles, Ryan Giggs, Britney Spears). Try to change the panel every five minutes	Questions: What have you learnt about public speaking? What are the top tips for public speaking? How do you think you will use what been covered today to improve your public speaking?

	Intro/ notes/ resources	Starter	Development	Plenary
Week 2		Show PowerPoint presentation (Name: Year 11 form time – speeches) Listen to speeches by Martin Luther King and Ghandi What do you notice about these two speeches?	Class discussion – Top ten ideas for handling questions and answers One pupil to be called to the front of the class and present a short speech about why they believe/don't believe in one of the statements below. After the speech the rest of the class to ask questions to the pupil in the spotlight! (rotate pupils with statements): • Rap music should be banned • Girls are just as good at boys at sports • Husbands should be allowed to have more than one wife • Britain should get rid of the royal family • Children under 16 years should not be given chocolate • Girls are brighter than boys • Is there such a thing as a superior race? • Health, wealth or love—which matters to you and why? • Men are from Mars; women are from Venus. What are your thoughts? • Do you think that space travel is a good idea and will you go? Why? • Do you think it is fair to have seven wives? Why? • Do you think the Queen should step down and Prince Charles should be King? Why? • The film *Alive* was the true story of a rugby team whose aeroplane crashed into the Andes and the only way for them to survive was through cannibalism—what are your thoughts? • Are schools responsible for teaching good manners? • Do you think that parents should be punished for their children's hooliganism? • Do you think there is too much emphasis on physical appearance? Why? • Should Prince Harry be sent to the front line? Why?	What are the top tips for handling questions and answers? What did you do well today? What must you do to improve next time?

	Intro/ notes/ resources	Starter	Development	Plenary
Week 3		Pupil comes to the front of the class and the rest of the class has the opportunity to ask interview questions to that pupil. Rotate every two minutes	Class discussion – Interview technique In pairs, discuss possible questions you could be asked in a college interview. Feedback to class Practise question and answers. Share with class	What are the key things to remember when going for an interview?
Week 4	Random objects	One pupil to stand at the front of the class and be an archaeologist expert with an ancient item (e.g. keys). Pupil to attempt to convince the class that the item is an ancient object through description (e.g. earrings worn by Cleopatra). Class to ask questions	Class discussion – Top ten ideas for getting rid of nerves In pairs, pupils to act out a successful interview scenario, referring back to notes from last week. Perform to class As a class, discuss strengths and areas to develop of performances. Choose the strongest performance for next week's inter-form competition Suggested inter-form competition to be judged next week: best interview scenario from each form presented to year group in an assembly. The winning act will receive a prize	Why is it important to overcome nerves? What general things can you do to overcome nerves?
Week 5			Discuss the competition – Strengths of performances Discuss the benefits of working in groups of three to act out interview scenarios (each taking on a role: interviewer, interviewee, observer, and expectations of each student in that role) In groups of three (interviewer, interviewee, observer) act out a successful interview scenario, referring back to the notes from last week. Rotate so that each person in the group takes on every role As a form, discuss strengths and weaknesses of performances in triads Next week – Mock interviews (head of year will present pupils with attendance and punctuality records, references)	What did you learn from this morning's competition?

	Intro/ notes/ resources	Starter	Development	Plenary
Week 6			Mock interviews – In front of whole class (pupil information from head of year)	What have you learnt about yourself and about public speaking over the last six weeks?

At the end of the unit we gave out the following:

Pupil feedback – Public speaking unit in form time

Name:

Tick the answer which you think applies to you.

1. Do I understand the importance of oracy?

   - ❏ YES
   - ❏ NO
   - ❏ UNSURE

2. Do I feel my confidence in speaking has improved?

   - ❏ YES
   - ❏ NO
   - ❏ UNSURE

3. Am I aware of public speaking techniques to boost my talking?

   - ❏ YES
   - ❏ NO
   - ❏ UNSURE

3. What have I learnt from this unit?

4. How do I feel about my learning of this unit?

   - ❏ SAD
   - ❏ CONFUSED
   - ❏ HAPPY

5. Why?

_____

_____

_____

Thank you.

Staff feedback – Public speaking unit in form time

Name:

1. What do you think the strengths of the unit are?

    _____

    _____

2. What are the areas that need developing?

    _____

    _____

3. Do you think the students have benefited from this unit?

    _____

    _____

4. Do you think you have benefited as a teacher from teaching this unit?

    _____

    _____

5. Any other points?

    _____

    _____

Thank you.

What alternatives are there?

➤ Allow thinking aloud time so students can have the opportunity to shape and solidify ideas. Plan activities so students can practice and develop speaking skills because they need opportunities to describe, explain and justify what they have learnt.

➤ In order for talking to be effective, it needs to be structured so that students are clear about the outcomes.

➤ Oral starters and plenaries are an effective and engaging way to allow students to expand their subject-specific language—students would also benefit from teacher modelling.

➤ Include the development of speaking as part of the learning objectives, ensuring that these skills are made explicit to the class.

➤ Every half term students should evaluate their own speaking skills and create targets which will help them reach their potential.

➤ Remember, all of the above speaking skills should be reinforced in all subject areas.

Where next for the public speaking form time unit?

➤ All form tutors offered training in the teaching of this unit.

➤ Two students from each form trained to co-teach the unit with the form teacher.

➤ All forms to carry out the public speaking unit during form time.

➤ Heads of year to create their own schemes suited to the needs of their students.

➤ Evaluations from both staff and students.

The role of reading in developing and raising literacy

The more you read, the more things you know. The more you learn, the more places you'll go.

Dr Seuss (1904–91), American writer

Any book that helps a child to form a habit of reading, to make one of his deep and continuing needs, is good for him.

Maya Angelou (1928–), American poet

We all recognise the importance of reading but getting students to read can be challenging, especially if you want to create a reading culture among your students. *Imagine a school in which every child loved to read … loved to talk … loved to write … Begin the journey now … together we can make a difference.* So, in order to deal with this challenge we must answer the following questions:

- What are the problems for teachers regarding students' reading?
- What are the pitfalls for you as an individual teacher with students reading in your subject?
- What can be done to address this?

With regards to what can be done to address this, the following strategies have worked well:

- Many subjects in the curriculum have subject-specific words. Ensuring students understand these words will help them to improve their understanding of the subject.
- Ensuring students learn the meaning of word roots will help their understanding of subject-specific words.
- Try to have regular discussion periods in your lesson so students can discuss key words and use them in context correctly.
- It is vital that these words are reviewed regularly.
- Give enough time to identifying new words—especially for new topics.
- Display key words and provide list for students.
- It is important the students are reminded how to access the text—continuous reading, close reading, skimming and scanning.
- Remember to create engaging, clear activities which relate directly to the text being studied.
- Shared reading is a good way to introduce new or difficult texts.
- Set up reading clubs.
- Set up a buddy reading system during form times—use older pupils to buddy up with younger pupils.
- Greater use of computers.
- Get parents involved.
- Make reading fun—be creative!
- Promote the library—the role of the library should be at the heart of the school.

My vision of learning for children and young people in the future has the library, in all its forms, at its heart.

Sir Timothy Brighouse (1940–), British educator

Did you know that 85% of secondary schools celebrate World Book Day?

Did you know that over 2,000 school libraries set up reading clubs in conjunction with the judging of the Carnegie and Kate Greenaway Medal book awards?

So, if your library is not already doing the following, they might be worth considering:

- Informs and promotes new texts to staff and students
- Book weeks
- Increases pupils' enjoyment of reading
- Workshops with authors
- Encourages creative thinking
- Celebrates cultural diversity
- Readathons
- Encourages wider reading and critical thinking.

> *The extent to which a school library can effectively meet the needs of learners and educators within the school is determined by the levels of collaboration with the rest of the school community.*
>
> *Start with the Child Report* (CILIP 2002)

Remember, the librarian must have the support of the rest of the school for your library to flourish. Your library should and could offer …

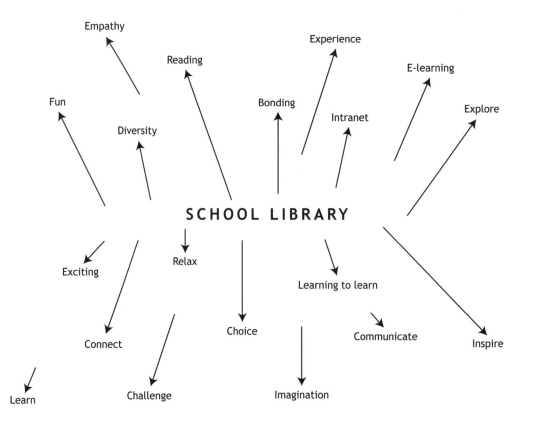

> *The way to get children reading is to leave the library door open and let them read anything and everything they want.*
>
> Terry Pratchett (1948–), British novelist

Become a Reading Connects school by visiting www.literacytrust.org.uk/readingconnects/index.html.

Remember to use the strategies in Chapter 2 to develop reading.

How can your subject promote reading through the use of the library?

	Workshops	Computers	Reading	Newspapers
English				
When? How?				
Maths				
When? How?				
Science				
When? How?				
Drama				
When? How?				
Music				
When? How?				
Art				
When? How?				
Geography				
When? How?				
History				
When? How?				
ICT				
When? How?				
Business				
When? How?				
D&T				
When? How?				
MFL				
When? How?				
RE				
When? How?				

The role of writing in developing and raising literacy

The pages are still blank, but there is a miraculous feeling of the words being there, written in invisible ink and claiming to become visible.

Vladimir Nabokov (1899–1977), Russian novelist

Research shows that a third of students' time is spent writing, which initially might seem like a benefit to their literacy skills. However, if they do not understand what they are writing, and it does not help them learn, then the effect will be negative. In the words of a Year 10 student:

You're copying things down from the book. You have been given ten minutes at the end of the lesson to do it. I thought I understood it but only when I was revising for my test I found out I didn't. I wished I had asked for help from the teacher but then I remembered there was not enough time because I was still copying when the bell went. I didn't read it and I don't understand it.

Writing does enhance learning but we must ensure: that the purpose is made clear to students; students make choices about their writing style, ensuring that it helps reflect the organisation of their thinking; and students are encouraged to write for many different purposes and audiences so that it supports the objectives of the lesson. Remember to remind students that they are merely building on the work they did in primary school—this is just the next step.

It is worthwhile asking your team to think about a Year 7, 8 or 9 lesson they have taught over the last week:

- What proportion of time was devoted to writing?
- Were all homeworks written tasks?
- What were the purposes of the writing?

Ask your staff to fill out the proformas (below) about the text types they use in their writing styles (the ones on the proforma are just a few of the possible choices—any additional ones can be added).

Questions/worksheets   ⟶   To ensure understanding

Note making/spider diagrams ⟶ To aid revision

Investigations   ⟶
- Learning how to collect valid results
- Learning how to carry out procedure
- Learning how to assess planning

Observations – in written form conclusions (experiments) ⟶
- Learning how to develop writing skills and to reveal evidence and reasoning
- Reveals recording of evidence

Now ask your team to complete other writing types which suit your subject.

Have a look at the strategies for literacy teaching in Chapter 2—there are some exciting ideas which have helped students improve their writing in all subjects. Remember to have fun and be creative with them!

Which text types does your subject use? Do your students have the writing frames?

Tick your subject's writing types in the boxes.

	Inform	Explain	Describe	Imagine	Entertain	Explore	Review	Analyse	Comment	Discuss	Argue	Persuade	Advise	Recount	Experiment	Information	Instruction
English																	
Maths																	
Science																	
Drama																	
Music																	
Art																	
Geography																	
History																	
ICT																	
Business																	
D&T																	
MFL																	
RE																	

■ Word frame to help students understand key words in text

This word frame is to help you when you are reading a new text. Write down the words that you think are important and those that you do not understand. Then look up the word/s in your dictionary to check the meaning, filling out the chart below … and watch your vocabulary grow …

Important words in text	Tick whether … unknown words	Tick whether … unsure of meaning	Tick whether … understand meaning	Meaning of word – dictionary definition

■ Writing frame – to help understanding of text

What have I already learnt about this subject?	Questions that need answering?	How am I going to answer the question asked?	Answer?

The role of EAL in transforming literacy

To have another language is to possess a second soul.

Charlemagne/Charles the Great (747–814), King of the Franks

Important factors for English as an additional language (EAL) learners is that they can extend their English through contact with other children and teachers, and often they learn quickly, especially if they are young enough. As teachers we should ensure that our lessons are designed to develop language; our classrooms are like shop windows selling language skills and we must make certain that the curriculum is inclusive to all.

The basic interpersonal communication skills, for the majority of us, develop between the ages of 2 and 3 years, whereas our cognitive academic language proficiency skills tend to develop between 5 and 8 years.

If we break down the stages of language development they are as follows:

- Beginners – students understand/speak little or no English.
- Developing beginner – students more able to communicate. Varying vocabulary and syntax.
- Developed beginner – lack of range in verbal and written English. Greater under-achievement in English and History.

So what strategies can we use?

- Set homework at the start of a lesson so that students can ask questions if they are unsure.
- Use teaching assistants.
- Provide a list of key words at the start of lesson.
- Encourage the use of phonics.
- Copying permitted from the board for revision purposes later.
- Use of bilingual and picture dictionaries.
- Allow students to use their own language—get students to write in English and translate. They could divide the page in half, so that half is English and half is their own language.
- Create a glossary.
- Present your subject in a simplified way—bullet points, differentiated worksheets, visuals, etc.
- Scaffolding and modelling
- We must continually monitor, assess and evaluate to ensure that progress is taking place.
- Support your EAL department by offering in-house training to staff.
- Use the literacy progress form from 'The role of writing in developing and raising literacy' (see above p. 147).
- Share good practice—ensure that all resources are easy to locate for everyone.
- Create a buddy system whereby EAL students can be matched up with fluent speakers and one lunchtime a week they are able to use the resources room to improve their English under the guidance of their fluent buddy.

Make your classroom inclusive:

- Promote learning to learn.

- Encourage talking and feedback.
- Be aware of the varying learning and literacy styles.
- Always go over the literacy skills and subject studied.
- Try to encourage collaborative work.
- Use fun, colourful and interesting written and visual resources.
- If you have an interactive whiteboard—use it. Have a look at 'Using ICT and media to develop students' literacy' (see above p. 131).

So let us end with a quote:

> *Language is the blood of the soul into which thoughts run and out of which they grow.*
>
> Oliver Wendell Holmes (1809–94), physician, lecturer and author

Remember to use the strategies in Chapter 2 to help your EAL students develop their literacy.

■ EAL student profile

Name: Date of birth:

Form: Targets:

	Date	Unable	Usually	Fluent	Notes
Speaking					
Can answer simple questions					
Can speak audibly					
Can make eye contact when speaking					
Can say the days of the week/months of the year					
Can count numbers in order					
Can tell the time - 12 hour clock					
Can understand school timetable					
Can name 50 objects in English					
Can talk about him/herself					
Can ask for help					
Listening					
Can listen attentively					
Reading					
Can say the alphabet phonetically					
Can comprehend words on sight					
Is familiar with -sh, -ch, etc.					

	Date	Unable	Usually	Fluent	Notes
Can respond to simple written statements					
Can understand diagrams/charts					
Writing					
Is able to copy English					
Is able to write some English					
Is able to write using capital letters and full stops					
Can use capital letters correctly					

Level 3 learners and transforming their learning through literacy

All children must achieve a good grasp of literacy and basic skills early on as the foundation for learning throughout life.

National Commission on Education, *Learning to Succeed* (1993)

Level 3 learners are those which are a worry for most of us. They should make the progress they need to succeed, but without that extra input there is a real possibility that they won't.

Often level 3 learners struggle because their reading age is below their chronological age; their vocabulary is narrow and spelling limited; accessing the curriculum is often demanding; they are inclined to rely on one reading strategy; their writing often needs writing frames; and their organisation needs work. All of these often result in many students feeling irritated which can lead to overdependence on support and behaviour issues.

The first thing is to ask yourself and your team are the following questions:

- What does being a level 3 learner mean to you?
- What are the issues they face?
- What are the issues we as teachers face?
- What intervention do they need?
- What support do we need?

It is important that each subject must make clear to the students the literacy skills being learnt through reading, writing and speaking. It is only by reinforcing them in each subject and stressing their importance that students will be able to transfer those skills across from one subject to the next.

The ways forward are as follows: identify the students, assess their needs and set targets for them. All teachers must differentiate in lessons to ensure that these targets can be met. Regular assessment of progress against targets must be carried out and new targets put in place when needed.

Remember, the generic strategies in Chapter 2 are tried and tested ways to help your students develop and become confident in literacy!

■ Literacy progress form

Student name:

Literacy needs:

Targets:

Subject	Date	Target studied in lesson	Student evaluation of literacy target learnt in lesson	Teacher evaluation of literacy target learnt in lesson (include strategies to help, if necessary)
English				
Maths				
Science				
Art				
Music				
Drama				
RE				
History				
Geography				
ICT				
Business				
MFL				
D&T				

The role of parents in transforming literacy

Literacy is, or ought to be, a shared responsibility.

John Hertrich in *Secondary Literacy: A Survey by HMI* (1998)

Whether we like it or not, we are shaped by our experiences as a child. Our home lives play a huge part, particularly as young children, on our habits and 'issues' as we grow up. So, it is vital that parents give their child the maximum head start by laying down the paving stones that will allow them to succeed in the world of education and then in life. Research carried out tells us:

- Parents who create high quality home learning environments engage regularly in activities that stretch a child's mind (Sylva et al. 2004).

- Children gain skills at home but also absorb a positive attitude and enthusiasm for learning. Parental involvement has an impact across all ethnic groups and social classes (Desforges and Abouchaar 2003).

- Fathers' interest and involvement has an independent effect on the improvement of children's literacy levels. Likewise, a mother's interest and involvement in her child's literacy development will be of benefit to the child (Goldman 2005).

It has been proven that parents reading to their children has a strong correlation to school success. The reason for this is that reading with parents can become an everyday occurrence and is therefore deemed 'safe'. If children are being read to every day this becomes the norm and so they want to continue with it. In addition, to have a parent read to a child means that dialogue will happen as questions, comments and conversation occur. In the words of Sir Winston Churchill: 'We shall succeed together and fail separately.'

What can schools do to encourage this to happen? Well, firstly the following questions need to be answered: What involvement do you have with parents? What effective involvement could you have with parents to boost literacy?

In answering these questions we must be aware of the following challenges which will need to be addressed:

- Time
- Confidence
- Understanding
- Language and literacy skills
- Attitudes towards school and others
- Other factors—poverty, disability, depression.

So what can we do?

All schools have different relationships with parents but perhaps the following will work for your school. Ensure that parents and children come together as one unit for the following:

- Parents are offered the opportunity to use the library to read to their children before or after school.
- Dads and sons who are having difficulties with literacy are invited to a 'common room' where they can read and write (emphasis on the social, with food provided).
- Parents and children are invited to join the school book club. Each half term a different book is read and parents with children are invited in to discuss the story.

- Parent and student literacy newsletter/magazine with literacy competitions for parents and children.
- Blog for families (parents and children) to share literacy skills and strategies to develop.
- Literacy evening—immerse both parents and children in literacy skills. Make it fun!
- Have a parent and student joint committee to raise literacy standards in school.
- Invite in speakers once every half term who have overcome literacy issues to succeed in life—invite parents and children.
- Have a literacy conference and invite other schools to attend along with parents and students. Contentious but make it a weekend so more parents will be available to attend.

Support websites

- www.bbc.co.uk/parenting – the BBC offers general parenting support.
- www.direct.gov.uk/EducationAndLearning/EarlyLearningForUnderFives/ HelpingYourChildToLearn/fs/en – the official government website Directgov offers advice on helping your child to learn and improving literacy. It also has links to the National Literacy Trust and Booktrust.
- www.literacytrust.org.uk/familyreading/parents/dads.html – the Family Reading Campaign offers fathers advice and strategies on how they can be involved with reading and what they can do to help their children.
- www.homedad.org.uk – this site links to other parenting sites and is aimed at fathers who stay at home.
- www.parentlineplus.org.uk – Parentline Plus offers advice on ways to help your child learn.

Boys and literacy

> *What are little boys made of?*
> *'Snips and snails, and puppy dogs tails*
> *That's what little boys are made of!'*
> *What are little girls made of?*
> *'Sugar and spice and all things nice*
> *That's what little girls are made of!'*
>
> Robert Southey (1774–1843), English poet

You'll be pleased, but not surprised, to hear that boys' media literacy is improving due to their motivation to engage in this type of literacy. So, by making literacy cool and fun we can hope to motivate boys and see improving results.

So what can we offer?

- A wide range of programmes, including subjects that are of particular interest to boys (New Zealand Education Review Office 2000).
- Boys can experience positive and productive forms of masculinity through competitive and individual work, through being encouraged to read at home and through making the classroom more boy friendly.

- Younger and Warrington in *Raising Boys' Achievement* (2005) state: 'Attempting to portray learning as "cool" and acceptable for boys—celebrating success so all boys want to learn, and no-one is embarrassed by not knowing the answer, needing extra help, or doing well.'

So what are the solutions?

What follows are some suggestions of possible solutions—but by no means is it exhaustive. It would be worthwhile brainstorming further ideas among your teams for ideas that are right for your school.

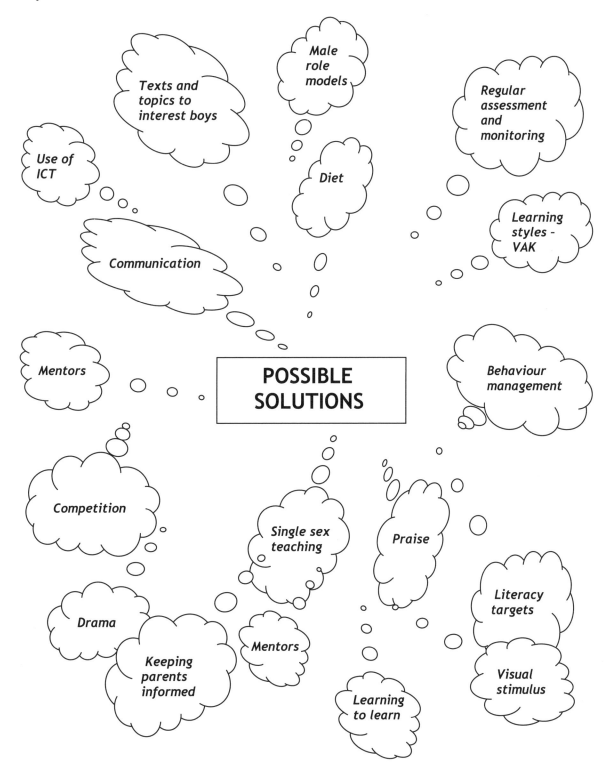

Some of the possible solutions include:

Single-sex teaching

Single-sex teaching appears most likely to be successful where staff are fully committed to it, where there is extensive preparation of staff and students before these groupings are put in place, where gender-specific teaching strategies are used and evolve, and where there is an ethos of achievement and discipline within the school.

(Younger and Warrington 2005)

Male-role models

Literacy is also promoted through non-traditional, hands-on approaches such as Internet use. Male role models from the local community are brought into the class not only to read to boys but also to underline the usefulness and importance of good literacy skills. Reactions from the boys taking part in the trial have been enthusiastic and positive.

(New Zealand Education Review Office 2000)

Assessment and monitoring

Boys need proportionately more feedback than girls to remain motivated and on-task.

(Redman et al. 2002)

Competition, competition, competition! Boys respond well to the competitive element.

Behaviour management

A high standard of behaviour management and discipline underpins effective strategies targeting boys.

(Younger and Warrington 2005)

Working with parents to get boys 'on side'—initiating meetings with parents of difficult boys and setting agreed parameters in relation to behaviour, using exclusions only as a very last resort.

(Younger and Warrington 2005)

Diet - you are what you eat

A lot of research has looked at food and its impact on learning and behaviour. Schools should look again at their canteens and tuck shops.

So where next?

The following have proved a huge success when we tried them:

- Involve male members of the family or older male pupil mentors.
- Establish a small cohort of boys in each year with literacy issues and work with them once a week to develop their literacy skills.

- Create displays of recent news items, books and magazines which would interest boys (e.g. Formula 1, cricket, football, cars). Male common area for these pupils to meet.
- Monthly evening meeting/social—informal but suggesting literacy targets. Opportunity to write or focus on lively writing and novels (*Face* by Benjamin Zephaniah, *Kes* by Barry Hines, etc.).

There are many possible strategies and solutions that may work for your school. Some you will need to adapt depending on the needs of your students, staff and parents. However, it is about persistence and keeping on reworking strategies until they suit the challenges of your school. Think of this as a springboard—the ideas to use initially before you shape your own and tailor them for your students.

Chapter 4
Generic Tools for Assessing Literacy

This chapter contains assessment materials to measure students' learning of literacy and the impact of literacy in our schools.

Student literacy self-assessment

Write down the literacy skills which *you feel you do well in,* under each one of the headings below—ask your teacher for help if necessary.

Speaking	Listening	Words	Reading	Writing

Write down the literacy skills which you feel *you need to improve* in, under each one of the headings below.

Speaking	Listening	Words	Reading	Writing

OK, so what targets can you set yourself?

What targets will you set yourself?	How will you achieve these targets?	When will you achieve these targets?	Comments

Thank you.

■ Marking the literacy criteria for this task

Student: Date:

Once you have written down the literacy criteria for the task you are writing, mark it. Remember to give a positive comment and set two literacy targets which will help you in the future.

Criteria	Positive comment	Targets

■ Shade in my literacy understanding at different stages of the task

Student: Date: Literacy skill to be assessed:

On being given the task ...

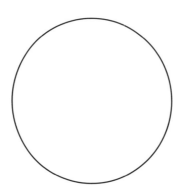

The shaded area of the circle equals the percentage of my understanding of the literacy skill.

During the task ...

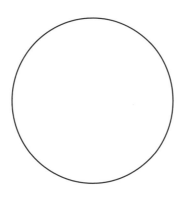

The shaded area of the circle equals the percentage of my understanding of the literacy skill.

After the task ...

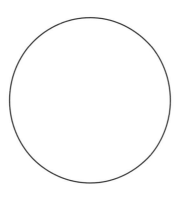

The shaded area of the circle equals the percentage of my understanding of the literacy skill.

■ Literacy assessment

What literacy skills have I used in this lesson?

_____

_____

What literacy skills did I learn/revise today?

_____

_____

When using this skill what must I remember to do?

_____

_____

What targets can I set myself so I practise using this skill?

_____

_____

What targets can I set myself so that I can do the best piece of work?

_____

_____

Any other comments?

_____

_____

Thank you.

■ What are my literacy concerns?

Write your literacy concerns in the bubble so that your teacher can help you.

■ Progression map for your students

As teachers we need to think about what literacy skills we want our students to achieve. In order to do this you will need to assess the students in each year group and produce your own literacy progression grid for what you want them to achieve in the four categories—speaking and listening, words, reading and writing.

■ Progression map of literacy skills - Speaking and listening

Speaking and listening	Year 7				Year 8				Year 9				Year 10				Year 11			
	Less able			More able	Less able			More able	Less able			More able	Less able			More able	Less able			More able

■ Progression map of literacy skills - Words

Reading	Year 7				Year 8				Year 9				Year 10				Year 11			
	Less able			More able	Less able			More able	Less able			More able	Less able			More able	Less able			More able

■ Progression map of literacy skills – Reading

Writing	Year 7		Year 8		Year 9		Year 10		Year 11	
	Less able	More able	Less able	More able	Less able	More able	Less able	More able	Less able	More able

■ Progression map of literacy skills – Writing

Words	Year 7		Year 8		Year 9		Year 10		Year 11	
	Less able	More able	Less able	More able	Less able	More able	Less able	More able	Less able	More able

Teacher literacy lesson observation

It is important to put in place strategies which will help staff members reach the literacy targets set by your school (e.g. courses, observations of other lessons, reading materials, copies of *The Literacy Toolkit*, etc).

Literacy lesson observations are meant to be supportive to staff and aid in their literacy professional development.

Staff: Observer: Date: Class:

Literacy focus:
Evidence:
Evidence of assessment:
Literacy wall displays:
Students' oral comments about the literacy skill focused on during this lesson:
Literacy targets for staff member:
How can we support you to attain these literacy targets?
Next observation date:

Bibliography

Abbot, J. and Ryan, T. (2000) *The Unfinished Revolution*. Stafford: Network Educational Press.

Appleyard, J. (1990) *Becoming a Reader: The Experience of Fiction from Childhood to Adulthood*. New York: Cambridge University Press.

Bailey, S. and Black, O. (2005) *The Mind Gym: Wake Your Mind Up*. London: Time Warner Books.

———— ———— (2006) *The Mind Gym: Give Me Time*. London: Time Warner Books.

Barthes, R. (1986) *The Responsibility of Forms: Critical Essays on Music, Art and Representation*, tr. R. Howard. Oxford: Basil Blackwell.

Bazalgette, C. (2004) 'The Shapes of Literacy: Media and the Future of English', *EnglishDramaMedia* 1: 5–10.

Bearne, E. (2003a) 'Rethinking Literacy: Communication, Representation and Text', *Reading: Literacy and Language* 37(3): 98–103.

—— (2003b) 'Ways of Knowing; Ways of Showing – Towards an Integrated Theory of Text', in M. Styles and E. Bearne (eds.) *Art, Narrative and Childhood*. Stoke-on-Trent: Trentham.

—— (2004) 'Multimodal Texts: What They Are and How Children use Them', in J. Evans (ed.) *Literacy Moves On*. London: David Fulton.

Bennett, J. (1991) *Learning to Read with Picture Books*. London: Thimble Press.

Bono, E. de (1993) *Teach Your Child to Think*. London: Penguin.

Bousted, M. and Öztürk, A. (2004) '"It Came Alive Outside My Head." Developing Literacies through Comparisons: The Reading of Classic Text and Moving Image', *Literacy* 38(1): 52–56.

British Film Institue (2002) *Moving Images in the Classroom*. London: BFI.

—— (2004) *Screening Shorts: Short Films to Develop Creativity, Literacy and Cineliteracy* (DVD). London: BFI.

—— and Parker, D. (2001) *Story Shorts: A Resource for Key Stage 2 Literacy*. London: BFI.

Brumfit, C. and Johnson, K. (eds.) (1979) *The Communicative Approach to Language Teaching*. Cambridge: Cambridge University Press.

Burn, A. (2004) 'Computer Games in English, Media and Drama', *EnglishDramaMedia* 2: 19–25.

Burnett, G (2002) *Learning to Learn*. Carmarthen: Crown House Publishing.

Butler, C. (2004) 'Using Film to Teach Reading Skills', *The Secondary English Magazine* 7(3): 16–19.

Butterfield, J. (2008) *The English Language Laid Bare*. Oxford: Oxford University Press.

Cairney, T. (2003) 'Literacy within Family Life', in N. Hall, J. Larson and J. Marsh (eds.), *Handbook of Early Childhood Literacy*. London: SAGE.

Carroll, L. (1865) *Alice's Adventures in Wonderland*. Macmillan.

Cartnell, D. and Whelehan, I. (eds.) (2002) *Adaptations from Text to Screen, Screen to Text*. London: Routledge.

Centre for Literacy in Primary Education (1991) *The Reading Book*. London: CLPE.

Chartered Institute of Library and Information Professionals (2002) *Start with the Child: Report of the CILIP Working Group on Library Provision for Children and Young People*. London: CILIP.

Christie, F. (2003) 'Writing the World', in N. Hall, J. Larson and J. Marsh (eds.), *Handbook of Early Childhood Literacy*. London: SAGE.

Claxton, G. (1998) *Building Learning Power*. Bristol: TLO.

——— (1998) *Hare Brain, Tortoise Mind*. London: Fourth Estate.

Comber, B. and Nixon, H. (2004) 'Children Reread and Rewrite their Local Neighbourhoods: Critical Literacies and Identity Work', in J. Evans (ed.), *Literacy Moves On*. London: David Fulton.

Considine, D. M. (1986) 'Visual Literacy and Children's Books: An Integrated Approach', *School Library Journal* 33: 38–42.

Covey, S. (1989) *The Seven Habits of Highly Successful People*. New York: Simon & Schuster.

Crowther, J., Hamilton, M. and Tett, L. (2001) *Powerful Literacies*. Leicester: National Institute of Adult and Continuing Education.

Department for Education and Employment (1998) *Secondary Literacy: A Survey by HMI*. London: HMSO.

Department for Education and Skills (1997) *The National Literacy Strategy*. London: QCA.

Department for Education and Skills (2007) *Secondary National Strategy*. London: QCA.

Desforges, C. and Abouchaar, A. (2003) *The Impact of Parental Involvement, Parental Support and Family Education on Pupil Achievement and Adjustment: A Literature Review*. London: DfES.

Dobson, H. (2004) 'Can Children Survive the NLS and Learn to Love Reading?' *The Secondary English Magazine* 8(1): 19–22.

Eliot, G. (1861) *Silas Marner*. William Blackwood and Sons.

Evans, J. (ed.) (2003) *Literacy Moves On*. London: David Fulton.

Fisher, R. (2004) 'Curiosity Kits: Linking Reading and Play in the Middle Years', in J. Evans (ed., *Literacy Moves On*. London: David Fulton.

Gardner, H. (1993) *Multiple Intelligences: The Theory in Practice*. New York: Basic Books.

——— (1999) *Intelligence Reframed*. New York: Basic Books.

Ginnis, P. (ed.) (1988) *The Trailblazers*. Nottingham: Education Now Books.

——— (2002) *The Teachers' Toolkit*. Carmarthen: Crown House Publishing.

——— and Ginnis, S. (2006) *Covering the Curriculum with Stories*. Carmarthen: Crown House Publishing.

Goldman, R. (2005) *Fathers' Involvement in their Children's Education*. London: NFPI.

Goodwyn, A. (2005) 'The Role of Media Education', in A. Goodwyn and J. Branson (eds.) *Teaching English: A Handbook for Primary and Secondary Teachers*. London and New York: RoutledgeFalmer.

——— and Branson, J. (eds.) (2005) *Teaching English*. London and New York: RoutledgeFalmer.

Gregorc, A. (2001). *Mind Styles: FAQs Book*. Columbia, CT: Gregorc Associates.

Hall, K. (2003) *Listening to Stephen Read: Multiple Perspectives on Literacy*. Buckingham: Open University Press.

Hall, N., Larson, J. and Marsh, J. (eds.) (2003) *Handbook of Early Childhood Literacy*. London: SAGE.

Hardy, B. (1977) 'Towards a Poetics of Fiction: An Approach through Narrative', in M. Meek, A. Warlow and G. Barton (eds.), *The Cool Web: The Pattern of Children's Reading*. London: Bodley Head.

Heath, S. B. (1983) *Ways with Words: Language, Life and Work in Communities and Classrooms*. Cambridge: Cambridge University Press.

Johnstone, K. (1979) *Impro: Improvisation and the Theatre*. London: Methuen.

Kenway, J. and Bullen, E. (2001) *Consuming Children: Education – Entertainment – Advertising*. Buckingham: Open University Press.

Kress G. (1997) *Before Writing: Rethinking the Paths to Literacy*. London: Routledge.

—— and Van Leeuwen, T. (1996) *Reading Images: The Grammar of Visual Design*. London: Routledge.

Labbo, L. and Reinking, D. (2003) 'Computers and Early Literacy Education' in N. Hall, J. Larson and J. Marsh (eds.), *Handbook of Early Childhood Literacy*. London: SAGE.

Lambirth, A. (2003) '"They Get Enough of that at Home": Understanding Aversion to Popular Culture in Schools', *Reading: Literacy and Learning* 37(1): 9–13.

Lucas, B. (2001) *Power Up Your Mind: Learn Faster, Work Smarter*. London: Nicholas Brealey.

—— (2005) *Discover Your Hidden Talents*. Stafford: Network Educational Press.

Luke, A. and Freebody, P. (1997) 'Shaping the Social Practices of Reading', in S. Muspratt, A. Luke and P. Freebody (eds.), *Constructing Critical Literacies*. New South Wales: Hampton Press.

Marsh, J. (2003) 'Early Childhood Literacy and Popular Culture', in N. Hall, J. Larson and J. Marsh (eds.), *Handbook of Early Childhood Literacy*. London: SAGE.

—— and Millard, E. (2000) *Literacy and Popular Culture: Using Children's Culture in the Classroom*. London: Paul Chapman.

McCloskey, B. (2005) 'A Wider Literacy: Media Education and the Moving Image in Northern Ireland', *EnglishDramaMedia* 3: 17–21.

McGuiness, D. (2005) *Language Development and Learning to Read: The Scientific Study of How Language Development Affects Reading Skills*. Cambridge, MA: MIT Press.

Mackey, M. (2002) *Literacies Across the Media: Playing the Text*. London: RoutledgeFalmer.

Marsh, J. (2003) 'Taboos, Tightropes and Trivial Pursuits: Pre-service and Newly Qualified Teachers' Beliefs and Practices in Relation to Popular Culture and Literacy'. Paper presented at AERA annual meeting, Chicago, April 2003.

Mascord, G. (2004) 'Update', *The Secondary English Magazine* 8(2): 5–6.

Masterson, P. and Button, O. (2005) 'Creating Your Own Learning to Learn Programme', in S. Percival (ed.), *Personalising Learning: Creative Approaches*. Bourne End: ALITE.

Meek, M. (1991) *On Being Literate*. London: Bodley Head.

Nation, K. and Snowling, M. (2004) 'Beyond Phonological Skills: Broader Language Skills Contribute to the Development of Reading', *Journal of Research in Reading* 27(4): 342–356.

National Commission on Education (1993) *Learning to Succeed*. London: Heinemann.

New Zealand Education Review (2000) *The Achievement of Boys*. Wellington: NZ.

Northern Ireland Film and Television Coummission/British Film Institute (2004) *A Wider Literacy: The Case for Moving Image Education in Northern Ireland*, available at www.niftc.co.uk

Ofsted (2002/3) *Curriculum Area Report – English*, available at www.ofsted.gov.uk

—— (2004/5) *Annual Report*, available at www.ofsted.gov.uk

Pinker, S. (1997) *How the Mind Works*. London: Viking/Allen Lane.

—— (2007) *The Stuff of Thought: Language as a Window into Human Nature*. London: Allen Lane.

Redman, P., et al. (2002) 'Boys Bonding: Same-Sex Friendship, the Unconscious and Heterosexual Masculinities', *Discourse* (Special issue: Retheorising Friendship in Educational Settings), 23(2): 179–191.

Qualifications and Curriculum Authority (2007) *The New National Curriculum*, available at www.standards.dcsf.gov.uk

Rodriguez, M. (1999) 'Home Literacy Experiences of Three Young Dominican Children in New York City', *Educators for Urban Minorities* 1(1): 19–31.

Sainsbury, M. and Schagen, I. (2004) 'Attitude to Reading at Ages Nine and Eleven', *Journal of Research in Reading* 27(4): 373–386.

Sara, A. (2006) Unpublished thesis.

Scott, D. (2004) Getting it Right for Children', in J. Evans (ed.), *Literacy Moves On.* London: David Fulton.

Smith, A. (2002) *The Brain's Behind It*. Stafford: Network Educational Press.

Spufford, F. (2002) *The Child That Books Built: A Life in Reading.* London: Faber and Faber.

Strang, J., Masterson, P. and Button, O. (2006) *ASK: How to Teach Learning-to-Learn in the Secondary School.* Carmarthen: Crown House Publishing.

Sylva, K., Melhuish, E., Sammons, P., Sivaj-Blatchford, I. and Taggart, B. (2004) *The Effective Provision of Pre-School Education (EPPE) Project. Technical Paper 12 – The Final Report: Effective Pre-School Education.* London: DfES/Institute of Education.

Unsworth, L. (2001) *Teaching Multiliteracies Across the Curriculum: Changing Contexts of Text and Images in Classroom Practice.* Buckingham: Open University Press.

Vasquez, V. (2004) 'Creating Opportunities for Critical Literacy with Young Children', in J. Evans (ed.), *Literacy Moves On.* London: David Fulton.

Vygotsky, L. (1962) *Thought and Language*, tr. E. Hanfmann and G. Vaker. Cambridge, MA: MIT Press.

Walker, B., (2000) *Diagnostic Teaching of Reading: Techniques for Instruction and Assessment.* 4th edition. New Jersey: Merrill.

Ward, S. (2000) *BabyTalk.* London: Century.

Waterland, L. (1988) *Read with Me: An Apprenticeship Approach to Reading.* London: Thimble Press.

Watson, W. and Styles, M. (1996) *Talking Pictures: Pictorial Texts and Young Readers.* London: Hodder and Stoughton.

Whelehan, I. (2002) 'Adaptations: The Contemporary Dilemmas', in D. Cartnell and I. Whelehan (eds.), *Adaptations from Text to Screen, Screen to Text.* London: Routledge.

Younger, M. and Warrington, M. (2005). *Raising Boys' Achievement.* DfES Research Report 636. London: DfES.

Index

Annotating **90**
Apostrophes **44–45**
Assessment 3, 10, 97, 105–107, 123–124, 127, 151, 155, 156, 163, 167
Attitude 12, 15, 17, 122, 133, 153, 171

Bearne, Eve 7, 9
Behaviour management 155–156
Book corners **61**
Boys 9, 154–157

Capital letters **22–23**
Cognitive-psychological perspective 4
Computers xiii, 7, 8, 10, 12, 27, 41, 55, 63, 130, 143, 145
Confidence 12, 13, 133–134, 153
Connectives **33–34**, 127
Cross-curricular literacy xviii, 123–124
Crosswords **63–64**

Dictionaries **24–25**, 27, 31, 36, 38, 46, 96, 130, 149

EAL 149–151
Every Child a Reader 8

Full stops **22–23**

Grammar 18, 122, 131

Herringbone Pattern **48–49**, 96
Homophones **30–32**

ICT 131
Imagination 5, 8, 13, 16
Internet 7, 9, 55, 131, 132, 156

Learning to learn 3, 21, 122, 127, 133, 135, 138, 144, 149, 155, 169, 171, 172
Level 3 learners 151
Listening 12, 14, 15, 95, 99, 100, 103–107, 109–111, 114, 115, 117, 126, 127, 133, 134, 150, 160, 165

Magazines 9, 61, 132, 157
Media literacy 10
Meek, Margaret 4, 5
Mentors 155, 156
Mobile phones 7, 8
Monitoring 122–127

Newspapers xiii, 4, 61, 132, 145
Notes **54**

Oracy 8, 123, 133–134

Paragraphs **41–43**
Parents 11, 22, 31, 36, 42, 122, 123, 131, 136, 139, 143, 153–154
Personalised learning 3, 10
Physiology 15
Praise 65, 127, 155
Prediction **57–58**
Presentations 93, **97–98**, 133–142
Primary Literacy Strategy 8
Proofreading 22, **46–47**
Psycho-linguistic perspective 4

Questions **55–56**, 112–113
Quotes **28–29**

Radio 14
Root words **20–21**

Scanning **59–60**, 143
Sentences 17, 18, 33–34, 41–42, **50–51**
Skimming **59–60**, 143
Socio-cultural perspective 4
Socio-political perspective 4
Speaking 4, 12, 14, 15, 95, 97, 104–107, 122, 123, 126, 127, 133–142, 150, 151, 160, 165
Speech **28–29**, 93, 110, 120, 126, 133, 135, 138, 139
Spelling 24–25, **26–27**, 129, 130
Story writing **91–92**
Student voice 127
Sudoku **63–64**

Teaching 4, 6, 8, 10–13, 18, 122, 124, 128, 129, 131, 136, 139, 142, 146, 149, 155, 156
Thesauruses **38–39**
Training 122–124, 128, 134, 142, 149

Vocabulary **35–37**, 149

Writing frames 75, 77, 79, 81, 84, 86, 88, 92
Writing 41–43, 50–51, 70–92, 146–149, 165, 166, 169